BAUDOUIN NGAH AKOH

DIPLOMACY, EXTREMISM AND DEVELOPMENT

The Triumph of Diplomacy: From Conflict Zones to Sustainable Futures

First edition

This book was professionally typeset on Reedsy.
Find out more at reedsy.com

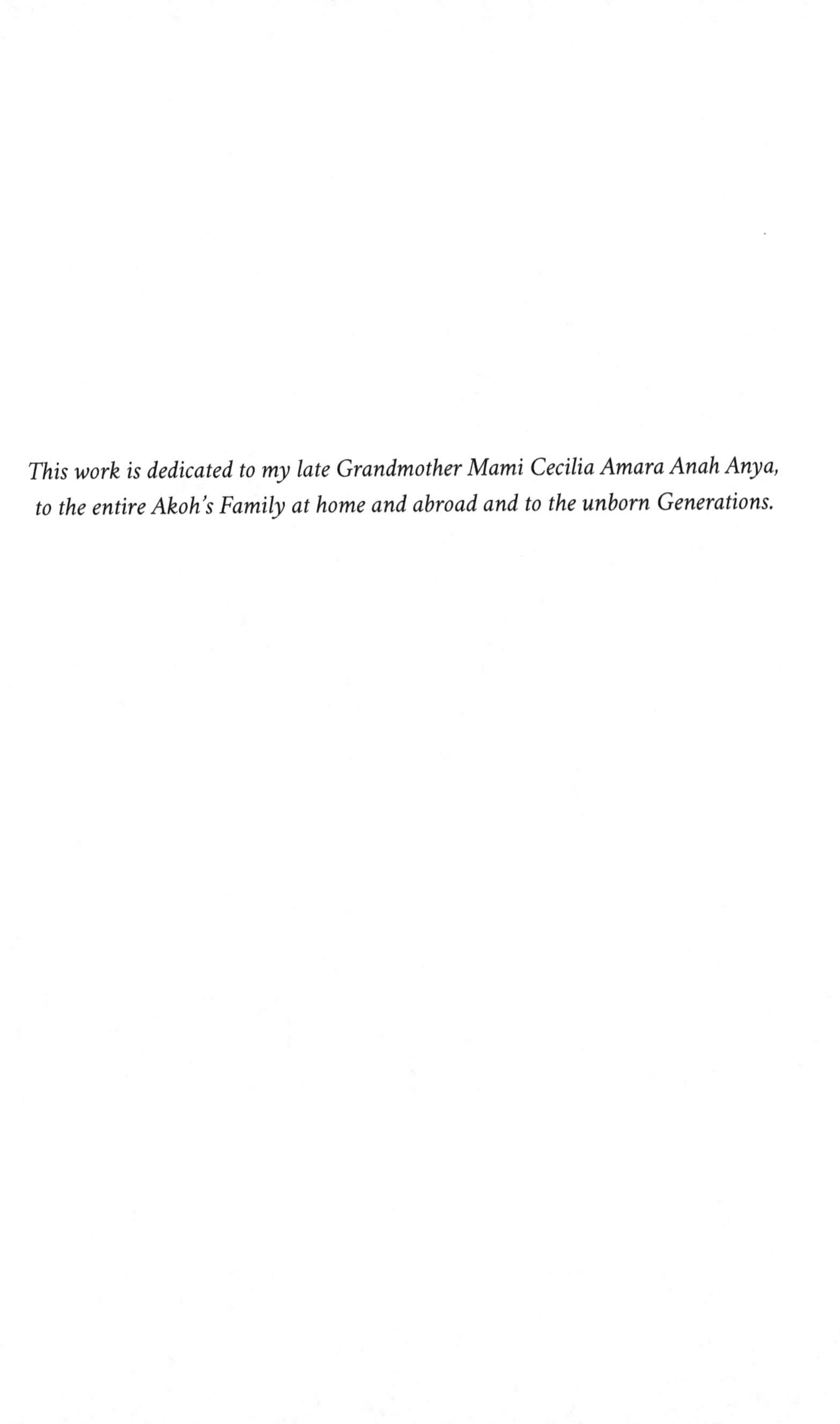

*This work is dedicated to my late Grandmother Mami Cecilia Amara Anah Anya,
to the entire Akoh's Family at home and abroad and to the unborn Generations.*

Contents

Preface

The book "Diplomacy, Extremism, and Development" is a comprehensive and insightful exploration of the intricate nexus of diplomacy, violent extremism, and development that shapes today's complex global landscape. The interconnectedness of these critical domains is explored, offering a roadmap to understanding the challenges and opportunities they present and how diplomacy can navigate these waters.

Chapter One: The Nexus of Diplomacy, Extremism, and Development, explores the conceptual foundations connecting diplomacy to dealing with challenges of violent extremism and development in our rapidly globalizing world. How diplomacy plays a pivotal role in addressing both challenges is explained.

Chapter Two: Underdevelopment, Violent Conflict, and Diplomacy discusses the underdevelopment-violent conflict nexus, explaining that underdeveloped regions are more susceptible to violent conflicts due to many factors, including economic disparities, weak governance, resource scarcity, and more. Diplomacy's role in conflict prevention and resolution is emphasized, showcasing its capacity to mitigate these challenges.

Chapter Three: Diplomacy's Role in Countering Extremism and Fostering Development, explains various diplomatic approaches, such as preventive diplomacy, good governance, cultural and educational diplomacy, and conflict resolution, all aimed at addressing violent extremism while fostering growth and stability.

Chapter Four: Diplomacy's Complex Pathways to Development and Security identifies and explains diplomatic approaches, chiefly bilateral diplomacy, partnerships, Track II diplomacy, and economic diplomacy, and how these diplomatic pathways contribute to development and security.

Chapter Five: Multilateral Diplomacy in Tackling Extremism and Development Challenges, discusses multilateral diplomacy, shedding light on the challenges and opportunities presented by international collaboration. Multilateralism's role in addressing the root causes of extremism and underdevelopment is highlighted.

Chapter Six: Future of Using Diplomacy to Address Extremism and Development Challenges explores emerging trends in diplomacy, especially the role of digital diplomacy, preventive diplomacy, and innovative financing models in addressing extremism and development challenges. The Chapter underscores the importance of adapting to emerging issues like online radicalization, climate change, and pandemics.

Chapter Seven: Firearms Proliferation: Impact, Human Rights, and Complex Challenges, examines the impact of firearms proliferation on violence, human rights, and development. From the weaponization of conflicts to the challenges of balancing security and human rights, the Chapter explains the multifaceted complexities surrounding this issue.

Chapter Eight: The Sahel Region's Complex Security and Humanitarian Challenges maps the complex security and humanitarian crises of the Sahel region. The epicenters of violence, the challenges faced by various countries, and the recent developments that have shaped the region's trajectory are discussed.

Chapter Nine: Silencing the Guns in Africa: Perspectives and Strategies for Peace and Development, presents summarily diverse perspectives from critical figures to provide insights into the "Silencing the Guns" initiative in Africa. Overall, the importance of regional and international commitment, inclusive peace processes, and addressing root causes to achieve peace and development on the continent are emphasized.

Chapter Ten: Arms Proliferation and the Global Impact of Transnational Organized Crime unravels the global impact of transnational organized crime, from drug trafficking to human smuggling, and how it intersects with arms proliferation and its impact on peace, human security, human rights, and development.

Chapter Eleven: Making Foreign Intervention More Rewarding: The

United States Global Fragility Act Strategy presents the objectives and comprehensive approach of the recent US legislation, emphasizing locally driven solutions, burden-sharing, and accountability.

Chapter Twelve: Recent Strategic Restructuring of Western Counterterrorism Architecture examines the strategic restructuring of Western counterterrorism architecture, including the European Union's Strategic Compass. The Chapter underscores the importance of adaptation, capacity-building, and a collaborative approach to ensure global security.

Chapter Thirteen: Jihadism - Learning from the Past and Adapting for the Future, identifies what lessons current approaches to countering Jihadism should render them more result-oriented and effective. Among other points, it is essential to distinguish between extremist groups, prioritize containment when necessary, and emphasize dialogue and conflict prevention in our approach.

Chapter Fourteen: Shifting Jihadism Landscape - A Comparative Analysis of IS and Al-Qaeda Strategies offers a comparative analysis of the strategies employed by the Islamic State (IS) and Al-Qaeda. The Chapter delves into their recruitment methods, expansionist approaches, and governance styles, highlighting their evolving nature.

Chapter Fifteen: Complexities of Countering the Fourth Wave of Jihadism discusses challenges posed by the fourth wave of Jihadism, limitations of traditional counterterrorism measures, and why addressing root causes, patient containment, engagement, and a comprehensive approach should be prioritized.

"Diplomacy, Extremism, and Development" invites you to explore the intricate interplay between diplomacy, violent extremism, and development. This book will provide insights into these complex issues and inspire us to engage with the pressing challenges of our time and contribute to a more peaceful and prosperous world.

INTRODUCTION

In a world marked by rapid globalization, shifting geopolitics, and the growing number of violent extremist hotspots, the connection between diplomacy, extremism, and development cannot be ignored easily. This book, "Diplomacy, Extremism, and Development," invites you to embark on a profound journey through the interwoven threads of these three critical domains that shape our global landscape. In a world where military action is rarely able to bring warring parties to live peacefully again, diplomacy becomes the quintessential bridge-builder, peacemaker, and catalyst for development. Diplomacy can play a vital role in confronting the challenges of violent extremism and fostering sustainable development.

As we explore this complex triad of diplomacy, extremism, and development, our journey will take us through the intricate web of theories, frameworks, and strategies that seek to decipher the interplay between these elements. We will also explore the root causes of extremism, the challenges of underdevelopment, and the multilayered strategies diplomacy employs to counter these threats.

Through the lens of diplomacy, we examine case studies and real-world scenarios demonstrating the power of negotiation, cooperation, and international alliances in addressing extremism and promoting development. We will seek to understand bilateral and multilateral diplomacy, showcasing how these diplomatic pathways are leveraged to prevent/resolve conflicts and promote peace and prosperity. Also, emerging trends in diplomacy, including the transformative potential of digital diplomacy, the imperative of preventive diplomacy, and the critical role of gender mainstreaming and cultural diplomacy in our ever-evolving world, are explored.

The perils of firearms proliferation, the complex security and humanitarian challenges facing the Sahel region, and the global impact of transnational organized crime are discussed. Moreover, it highlights the role of diplomacy as a tool to address these multifaceted issues.

In the following chapters, we will hear from esteemed voices offering their perspectives on silencing the guns in Africa, the complexities of countering the fourth wave of jihadism, and the strategic restructuring of Western counterterrorism architecture. These insights will provide a comprehensive view of the ever-changing landscape of diplomacy, extremism, and development. The author invites us to an immersion into the intricate tapestry of global affairs and diplomacy's pivotal role in shaping our world.

"Diplomacy, Extremism, and Development" is a guide to understanding the challenges and opportunities at the intersection of diplomacy, extremism, and development. It is a call to action, an exploration of possibilities, and an invitation to engage with the complex issues of our time. Welcome to this journey in search of a more peaceful and fast-developing world as we explore the nexus of diplomacy, counter-extremism, and development.

CHAPTER ONE: THE NEXUS OF DIPLOMACY EXTREMISM, AND DEVELOPMENT

Summary of Chapter One

1. The interconnectedness of Diplomacy, Violent Extremism, and Development: The interaction between diplomacy, violent extremism, and development is critical in today's global landscape characterized by rapid globalization and shifting geopolitics. Diplomacy plays a vital role in addressing the challenges of violent extremism and fostering sustainable development by preventing conflicts, promoting cooperation, and addressing root causes.

2. Economic Disparities and Extremist Recruitment: Economic disparities, lack of access to education, infrastructure deficits, youth unemployment, and involvement in illicit economies contribute to extremist recruitment. These factors hinder development and create conditions conducive to violent extremism.

3. Successful Use of Diplomacy: Diplomacy has successfully resolved violent extremism through peace agreements like the Good Friday Agreement, international mediation efforts, countering extremist narratives, humanitarian diplomacy, regional diplomacy, development diplomacy, cultural and educational diplomacy, and more.

4. Theories and Frameworks Linking Extremism and Development:

Various theories and frameworks, including the grievance theory, REC framework, development-extremism nexus framework, pull and push factors framework, systemic approach, resilience and community-based approach, and human development approach, provide insights into the complex interplay between violent extremism and development.

The Context of Diplomacy and Violent Extremism and Development

Diplomacy, violent extremism, and development are interconnected facets of the complex global landscape, especially now, an era characterized by rapid globalization, unprecedented technological advancements, and shifting geopolitical dynamics. The interaction between diplomacy, violent extremism, and development has become a critical focal point for governments, international organizations, scholars, and policymakers. As the art of skilful negotiation and peaceful resolution of conflicts, diplomacy is pivotal in addressing the challenges of violent extremism and fostering sustainable development. In a world where ideological divides, socioeconomic disparities, and religious or political radicalization can lead to violent expressions, diplomacy is vital to preventing and mitigating conflicts. Effective diplomacy can facilitate early dialogue and build trust that helps resolve conflicts among parties and encourage cooperation, thereby diminishing the root causes of extremism and promoting stability.

Violent extremism is a multifaceted threat that transcends borders and manifests in various forms, including terrorism, insurgency, and radical ideologies. The complex nature of this challenge requires a guided mix of military deterrence that is well informed by precise intelligence and wholesome diplomatic efforts to run down stubborn extremists, popularize empowering narratives to displace extremist propaganda, promote tolerance, and rehabilitate radicalized individuals. Violent extremism can truncate or adversely disrupt development. A region or country plagued by extremism often faces economic stagnation, social disintegration, and infrastructural deficits, hindering their progress and well-being.

Since development is a fundamental aspiration for nations and communities, its pursuit is intrinsically linked to diplomacy and counter-violent extremism efforts. Moreover, adequately defined development goals can serve as a pathway to address the underlying grievances that extremist groups exploit. Equally, diplomatic initiatives prioritizing peacebuilding should prioritize poverty alleviation, human capital development through improved healthcare and education, and promote economic opportunities, such that the tendency for the majority of the population to assist in extremist ideologies and fundamentalism is curtailed.

Building, sustaining/maintaining the healthy intersection of diplomacy, counter-extremism, and development demands a comprehensive and holistic approach, where government, the private sector, and civil society work together, actively fostering dialogue, conflict prevention, and socioeconomic progress. Hence, this book explores this delicate terrain into the intricate dynamics between diplomacy, violent extremism, and development, examining their interdependencies, challenges, and potential solutions to create a more peaceful and prosperous world for all.

Economic Disparities, Desperation and Extremist Recruitment

The interconnectedness between violent extremism and development manifests itself in several ways, often with profound implications for security and socioeconomic development. Below, we discuss a few cases to demonstrate how the factors interplay and possible outcomes.

High-Income Disparity – there are strong links between income disparity and violent extremism. For instance, in the Sahel region of Africa, extreme poverty and limited economic opportunities have contributed to the recruitment of militants by groups like Boko Haram and Al-Qaeda in the Islamic Maghreb (AQIM).

Lack of Access to Education - Limited access to quality education, especially for girls, can foster a sense of exclusion and frustration. The Taliban's ban on girls' education in Afghanistan exemplifies how a lack of educational opportunities can fuel extremism.

Infrastructure Deficits and State Legitimacy - Areas with limited or poor state presence, in terms of infrastructures and law enforcement institutions, are prone to extremism. The absence of significant government presence creates a power vacuum that extremist groups exploit. Somalia's instability, primarily due to a lack of governance and infrastructure, has allowed groups like Al-Shabaab to thrive.

Youth Unemployment and Radicalization - High unemployment rates, particularly among educated youth, can lead to frustration and alienation. This vulnerability has been exploited by groups like ISIS in Iraq and Syria, which attracted recruits from economically disadvantaged backgrounds.

Illicit Economies and Extremist Financing - Extremist groups often tap into illicit economies, such as drug trafficking or illegal mining, to fund their activities. The Taliban's involvement in the opium trade in Afghanistan is an example.

Resilience and Community Development - Engaging communities in development initiatives can build resilience against extremist ideologies. The "PVE/CVE" (Preventing Violent Extremism/Countering Violent Extremism) programs in various countries, including Kenya and Indonesia, have shown how community-led development can deter radicalization.

The interconnectedness between violent extremism and development is evident across various dimensions. Addressing this nexus requires a comprehensive approach that combines security measures with efforts to alleviate poverty, improve education, and promote inclusive development. A better understanding of this relationship is essential for formulating effective policies and interventions to counter extremism while fostering sustainable development and stability.

Examples of Successful Use of Diplomacy to Resolve Violent Extremism

Negotiating Peace Agreements – The Good Friday Agreement

The Good Friday Agreement in Northern Ireland (1998) involved intensive diplomatic efforts that led to a ceasefire and a comprehensive peace deal between the British and Irish governments and political parties representing Catholic and Protestant communities. The agreement ended decades of violence and laid the foundation for economic development and political stability in Northern Ireland.

International Mediation

International mediation has been instrumental in resolving conflicts in various regions. Diplomatic efforts by mediators like the United Nations, the African Union, and individual countries have helped bring warring parties in South Sudan, Bosnia and Herzegovina, and Mozambique (for instance) to the negotiating table. Successful mediation leading to peace agreements can engender the stability needed for development efforts to take root.

Countering Extremist Narratives Using Diplomacy

Diplomatic channels can be used to engage with countries that may inadvertently support extremist ideologies. For instance, the United States and its allies have pressured Gulf states to combat the financing of extremist groups. Reducing terrorism financing weakens their capacity to carry out acts of violence.

Humanitarian Diplomacy: Diplomatic initiatives can also serve to promote tolerance and reconciliation. In post-conflict societies, notably, diplomacy can support reconciliation processes. For example, South Africa's Truth and Reconciliation Commission, led by Archbishop Desmond Tutu, is a renowned example of diplomatic efforts to heal a divided nation. Such initiatives contribute to social cohesion and create an atmosphere where development can thrive.

Regional Diplomacy: Initiatives of regional organizations like ECOWAS played a crucial role in addressing extremism in the West African region. The establishment of the Multinational Joint Task Force to combat Boko Haram is a result of regional diplomatic cooperation. Regional diplomacy enhances collective security, fosters stability, and creates an environment conducive to development.

Development Diplomacy: Countries and regional blocs can negotiate for and secure international assistance for development projects in conflict-affected areas. The Tokyo International Conference on African Development (TICAD) is an example of a diplomatic initiative that promotes development in Africa. Development diplomacy helps rebuild infrastructure, provide education and healthcare, and address the root causes of extremism.

Cultural and Educational Diplomacy: Cultural and educational exchanges, facilitated through diplomacy, can promote understanding and tolerance among nations. The Fulbright Program, for instance, fosters people-to-people connections and promotes a positive image of the United States globally. Such exchanges can counter extremist narratives by building bridges between cultures and promoting peaceful dialogue.

In sum, diplomacy is a powerful tool for resolving violent extremism and supporting development. Negotiation, mediation, and various diplomatic initiatives can resolve conflicts and extremist ideologies, and the conditions for sustainable development can be established.

Theories/Frameworks Linking Violent Extremism and Development

Various theories/frameworks aim to understand/explain the linkages between violent extremism and development. These theories help illuminate the complex interplay between these two phenomena and provide insights into their interconnectedness. The prominent theories/frameworks linking violent extremism and development are presented below.

The Grievance Theory

The grievance theory posits that socioeconomic and political grievances, such as poverty, inequality, or political repression, are critical drivers of violent extremism. When individuals or communities perceive themselves as marginalized or oppressed, they may turn to extremist ideologies and violence to address their grievances. The Arab Spring uprisings in the Middle East and North Africa were driven, in part, by grievances related to unemployment, corruption, and political repression. Also, the ongoing Anglophone crisis in Cameroon can be linked to the grievances of the minority English-speaking population.

The Radicalization-Extremism-Counterterrorism (REC) Framework

This framework describes how individuals become radicalized, leading to extremism and terrorism. It considers multiple factors, including personal grievances, social networks, and ideological influence. For example, the process of radicalization leading to extremism and terrorism is often seen in cases where individuals are exposed to extremist ideologies online and then join extremist groups, such as ISIS or Al-Qaeda.

The Development-Extremism Nexus Framework

This framework emphasizes the two-way relationship between development and extremism. At the first level, underdevelopment can create conditions conducive to the rise of extremism; at the second, extremism can hinder development. For example, in Afghanistan, decades of conflict and insecurity have impeded development efforts, while the presence of extremist groups like the Taliban has further disrupted stability and development.

The Pull and Push Factors Framework

This framework identifies the "pull" factors that attract individuals to extremism (such as ideological beliefs or religious fanaticism) and "push" factors that drive individuals away from their communities (such as discrimination or persecution). The recruitment of foreign fighters by ISIS involved pull factors like the promise of a utopian Islamic state and push factors such as feelings of alienation in Western societies.

The Systemic Approach

The systemic approach considers the broader global and regional dynamics that influence violent extremism and development. It looks at factors like geopolitics, state fragility, and the role of international actors. The Syrian conflict is often analyzed using a systemic approach, considering the involvement of various regional and global powers and its impact on the conflict and its development in the region.

The Resilience and Community-Based Approach

This approach focuses on building resilience within communities to resist extremist ideologies and violence. It involves community engagement, social cohesion, and addressing the root causes of vulnerability. For example, Programs like the Strong Cities Network and community policing initiatives in various countries aim to build community resilience against extremism by fostering trust and cooperation.

The Human Development Approach

This approach considers development not only in terms of economic indicators but also in terms of human well-being. It argues that investments in education, healthcare, and social inclusion can reduce the appeal of extremism. For example, the United Nations' Sustainable Development

Goals (SDGs) encompass various dimensions of human development and seek to address the underlying factors that can contribute to extremism.

These theories and frameworks offer diverse perspectives on the linkages between violent extremism and development. Understanding these connections is crucial for policymakers and practitioners to design effective strategies that counter extremism and promote sustainable development and peace.

Characteristics and Drivers of Violence

Violence is generated through a complex interplay of individual, social, economic, and political factors. It can manifest in various forms, such as interpersonal violence, community conflicts, political violence, and terrorism. The characteristics and drivers of violence are explained below.

Interpersonal Violence

Domestic violence is a prevalent form of interpersonal violence worldwide. In this case, the violence typically occurs within families or intimate relationships. Perpetrators often exploit power imbalance to exert power and control over victims. Violence can be physical, psychological, or sexual and tends to occur repeatedly. Victims are often isolated from support networks and threatened, making it harder to escape the abusive relationship. Interpersonal violence follows a cycle of tension-building, explosion, and reconciliation, which can be difficult to break without intervention.

Community Conflicts

The ethnic conflict in Bosnia and Herzegovina in the 1990s is a notable example of a community conflict marked by violence. Community conflicts are often identity-based, often rooted in ethnic, religious, or cultural differences. Communities often become polarized, and violence escalates when individuals or groups perceive a threat to their identity or rights.

Most community conflicts have longstanding historical roots that resurge occasionally, making reconciliation challenging. External factors and geopolitical interests can exacerbate local conflicts.

Political Violence

The Syrian civil war is a significant example of political violence involving multiple parties, including the government, rebel groups, and foreign actors. It can have ideological roots, where political violence stems from ideological differences or competing visions of governance. It can be a form of armed conflict where armed groups and state forces engage in violent confrontations. It can also cause displacement, causing massive refugee flows and internally displaced populations. Multiple actors, including state and non-state, are often involved, making resolution challenging.

Terrorism

The 9/11 terrorist attacks in the United States by Al-Qaeda illustrate modern international terrorism. Terrorism can be informed by political goals, where terrorist groups seek to achieve political or ideological objectives through violence. It can take the form of indiscriminate targeting, where terrorists aim at surprise attacks, mainly on soft targets, aiming to create fear and disrupt society. Terrorism can also take the form of transnational networks, making counterterrorism efforts in individual countries largely ineffective. Terrorism can involve propaganda and recruitment, exploiting social media for online radicalization and recruitment.

Gang Violence

Gang violence in Central America, particularly in countries like El Salvador and Honduras, is a prominent example. Many power gangs vie for control over specific neighbourhoods or territories. Violence is linked to criminal activities such as drug trafficking, extortion, and organized crime.

Gangs frequently recruit and exploit vulnerable youth, and gang violence contributes to social instability and undermines community cohesion.

Hate Crimes

The Christchurch Mosque shootings in New Zealand (2019) exemplify hate-motivated violence. Hate crimes target individuals or groups based on race, religion, ethnicity, or gender. In most cases, perpetrators are influenced by extremist ideologies or hate groups. Hate crimes can create fear and division within communities.

Structural Violence

The persistence of extreme poverty and inequality in many parts of the world is an example of structural violence. Most structural violence incidences result from systemic injustice: Structural violence results from social, economic, or political systems that systematically harm marginalized groups. It may not involve direct physical violence but causes harm through deprivation, discrimination, or lack of access to basic needs. Structural violence can perpetuate cycles of poverty and inequality, leading to social unrest.

In summary, violence exhibits diverse characteristics depending on its context and causes. It can result from personal grievances, identity-based conflicts, political ideologies, or systemic injustices. Understanding these characteristics is essential for developing effective strategies to prevent and address violence.

Review Questions

1. How does diplomacy contribute to countering violent extremism and promoting development?
2. What are some examples of regions where economic disparities have led to extremist recruitment?

3. How has diplomacy been used to counter extremist narratives?
4. What are the fundamental theories/frameworks explaining the link between violent extremism and development?
5. What are the characteristics and drivers of violence in various contexts?
6. Provide examples of successful regional diplomatic initiatives in countering extremism and promoting development.

Discussion Points

1. Explore the role of cultural and educational diplomacy in promoting tolerance and countering extremist ideologies.
2. Discuss the challenges and opportunities of using development diplomacy to address the root causes of extremism in conflict-affected regions.
3. Analyze the impact of economic disparities on the recruitment of extremists and its consequences for development.
4. Debate the effectiveness of different theories and frameworks in understanding and addressing the nexus between violent extremism and development.
5. Discuss humanitarian diplomacy's ethical and practical considerations in post-conflict reconciliation processes.

CHAPTER TWO: UNDERDEVELOPMENT, VIOLENT CONFLICT, AND DIPLOMACY

Summary of Chapter Two

1. Underdevelopment-Violent Conflict Nexus: Underdeveloped regions are more prone to violent conflicts due to economic disparities, social and ethnic diversity, weak governance, resource scarcity, political instability, external interventions, and inadequate access to education and information. These factors interact and reinforce each other, leading to heightened instability and violence.

2. Examples of Violent Hotspots and Development Deterioration: Conflict-ridden regions like Syria, Yemen, the Democratic Republic of Congo (DRC), Afghanistan, and South Sudan have experienced severe development deterioration, including infrastructure destruction, displacement crises, economic collapse, and healthcare and education system disruptions.

3. Role of Diplomacy in Addressing Extremism and Promoting Development: Diplomacy plays a crucial role in conflict prevention and resolution, countering extremist narratives, fostering regional and multilateral cooperation, securing development assistance, facilitating conflict transformation, delivering humanitarian aid, and promoting peacebuilding and reconciliation.

4. Theories Relevant to Diplomacy for Conflict Resolution: Various diplomatic theories and approaches, including realism, liberalism, constructivism, game theory, the diplomacy of restraint, Track I, Track II, and Track III diplomacy, the diplomacy of small states, crisis diplomacy, public diplomacy, and soft power diplomacy, offer diverse perspectives and strategies for conflict resolution.

The Underdevelopment – Violent Conflict Nexus

Violent conflicts tend to be more predominant in underdeveloped regions of the world due to a combination of factors that create fertile ground for conflict. These factors interact and reinforce each other, leading to heightened instability and violence. Important justifications for the underdevelopment-violent conflict nexus are provided below.

Economic Factors

The violent conflicts in Sub-Saharan Africa (SSA) are primarily linked to resource sharing, linked to what is sometimes described as the "resource curse" thesis. In particular, the conflicts in the DRC, South Sudan, and Nigeria's Niger Delta region are linked to the struggle for resource control. Underdeveloped regions often face high poverty levels, unemployment, and income inequality. A lack of economic opportunities can lead to grievances as people struggle to meet their basic needs, creating a pool of potential recruits for armed groups and insurgencies.

Social and Ethnic Diversity

The Balkans, for example, witnessed ethnic conflicts, such as the Bosnian War, where historical animosities among different ethnic groups escalated into violence. Underdeveloped regions often have diverse populations with varying ethnic, religious, and cultural backgrounds. This diversity can create tension and conflict as different groups vie for power and resources when coupled with limited access to education and economic resources.

Weak Governance and Corruption

The crisis in Afghanistan was mainly linked to weak governance and corruption. More generally, underdeveloped regions often have fragile or corrupt governments that fail to provide essential services, enforce the rule of law, or address grievances, thus creating a power vacuum and encouraging the emergence of armed groups, militias, and warlords who challenge state authority.

Resource Scarcity and Competition

The conflict in Darfur, Sudan, was partly driven by competition over water and grazing lands. A similar situation occurs in the Sahel region, where desertification reduces available fodder for cattle and pushes herders into traditional farmlands. Generally, limited access to essential resources like water, arable land, and pastures can intensify competition and disputes, especially in regions where resource management is poorly regulated, causing violent conflicts between communities or ethnic groups.

Political Instability and Authoritarianism

The Arab Spring uprisings that swept across several underdeveloped Arab countries, including Tunisia, Egypt, and Syria, were driven by political instability. Many underdeveloped regions experience political instability due to authoritarian regimes, lack of political representation, or flawed electoral processes. These conditions can lead to mass protests, uprisings, and, in some cases, civil wars.

External Interventions and Geopolitical Interests

The Cold War rivalry between the defunct USSR and the US fueled proxy wars in underdeveloped regions like Afghanistan and Central America. Underdeveloped regions often become battlegrounds for proxy wars between the international powers pursuing their geopolitical interests. External interventions can exacerbate or create new conflicts, making the situation more volatile.

Inadequate Access to Education and Information

The Lord's Resistance Army conflict in Uganda recruited child soldiers, exploiting their lack of education and access to information. Underdeveloped regions often have limited access to quality education and information, which makes the population more susceptible to manipulation by extremist groups who offer a sense of purpose and belonging.

Generally, underdeveloped regions of the world are prone to experiencing a vicious cycle of poverty, political instability, and conflict. These regions are more vulnerable to violent conflicts due to economic, social, political, and environmental factors that interact and reinforce each other. Addressing these underlying issues and promoting development is crucial for reducing the preponderance of violence in such areas.

Examples of Violent Hotspots and Their Development Deterioration

Syria

Syria has been marred by a brutal civil war since 2011, with multiple armed groups, including the Syrian government, rebel forces, and extremist organizations, clashing for control. Development deterioration has been experienced in different areas, including:

Infrastructure Destruction: Much of the infrastructure, including schools, hospitals, and water facilities, was severely damaged or destroyed, hampering development efforts.

Displacement Crisis: Millions of Syrians were internally displaced or forced to seek refuge abroad, straining resources and hindering social and economic progress.

Economic Collapse: The Syrian economy collapsed, with soaring unemployment and a significant decline in GDP, resulting in widespread poverty and food insecurity.

Yemen

Yemen has experienced a protracted civil war and conflict since 2015, with Houthi rebels clashing with the Yemeni government and Saudi-led coalition forces. Development deterioration is predominantly experienced in the areas of:

Humanitarian Crisis: Yemen faces one of the world's worst humanitarian crises, with millions needing food, water, and medical assistance.

Health and Education Systems Collapse: The conflict has severely impacted health and education systems, with many schools and healthcare facilities damaged or closed.

Economic Decline: The conflict has caused a sharp economic decline, exacerbating poverty and unemployment, while the currency has depreciated, causing skyrocketing prices of essential goods.

Democratic Republic of Congo (DRC)

The eastern regions of the DRC, including North and South Kivu, have experienced ongoing conflict involving various rebel groups, militias, and government forces. Development deterioration involves:

Displacement and Insecurity: Persistent conflict has led to widespread displacement, disrupted agriculture, and created insecurity, making it challenging for communities to recover and develop.

Resource Exploitation: The DRC's rich mineral resources have fueled conflict and exploitation, diverting resources from development projects.

Weak Governance: Corruption, weak state institutions, and a lack of effective governance have hindered development efforts in the region.

Afghanistan

Afghanistan experienced decades of conflict, with the Afghan government, Taliban, and other armed groups involved in a protracted war. Development deterioration involves:

Education and Healthcare Challenges: The conflict has disrupted education and healthcare services, particularly in rural areas, affecting human capital development.

Economic Instability: Ongoing violence has hindered economic growth and development, as investors are wary of investing in an unstable environment.

Displacement and Refugee Crisis: Afghanistan has one of the largest populations of internally displaced persons and refugees, creating social and economic challenges in nneighbouringcountries.

South Sudan

South Sudan, which gained independence in 2011, plunged into a civil war in 2013, with ethnic and political tensions leading to conflict. The crisis denied the new country an opportunity to initiate meaningful growth and development programs, causing the following deteriorations:

Fragile State Institutions: The conflict has impeded the establishment of stable state institutions, including security forces, leading to continued instability.

Food Insecurity: The conflict has disrupted agriculture and displaced communities, resulting in food insecurity and malnutrition.

Education Disruption: Many schools have been closed or repurposed for military use, limiting access to education and human capital development.

Generally, violent conflict causes destruction and adversely affects development in infrastructure, healthcare, education, and the overall economy. These regions' persistent instability and violence have hindered progress and led to humanitarian crises, emphasizing the critical need for conflict resolution and sustainable development efforts.

How Diplomacy Can Help to Address Extremism and Promote Development

Diplomacy can check violent extremism and promote development in various ways. As the practice of engaging in negotiations, dialogue, and international relations, diplomacy can help get rival parties talking meaningfully and, by so doing, prevent and or mitigate violent extremism while fostering sustainable development. The critical roles of diplomacy in counter-extremism and development are explained below:

Conflict Prevention and Resolution

Diplomatic efforts can help mediate conflicts and bring warring parties to the negotiating table. For example, the peace negotiations between the government and the Revolutionary Armed Forces of Colombia (FARC) in Colombia were facilitated by diplomacy, leading to a historic peace agreement. Diplomacy can also help to prevent conflicts from escalating into violent extremism by addressing root causes, reducing tensions, and finding peaceful resolutions.

Countering Extremist Narratives

Extremist narratives can be countered through diplomatic engagement, which involves building relationships and engaging with countries where extremist ideologies thrive. Diplomatic channels can be used to counter extremist narratives and ideologies through dialogue and persuasion. There is also Soft Power Diplomacy, whereby parties can engage in cultural exchanges, educational programs, and public diplomacy efforts to promote tolerance, understanding, and counter-radicalization.

Regional and Multilateral Cooperation

Diplomacy can foster regional alliances and cooperation to address cross-border extremist threats. For instance, the Global Counterterrorism Forum (GCTF) is a diplomatic initiative to enhance international cooperation on counterterrorism efforts. Also, multilateral diplomacy involving international organizations like the United Nations (UN) is central in facilitating diplomacy among member states to address violent extremism and promote development through initiatives like the Sustainable Development Goals (SDGs).

Development Diplomacy

Diplomacy is crucial in negotiating and disbursing foreign aid and development assistance. Diplomatic efforts can secure funding and resources for development projects in regions affected by extremism. Moreover, diplomats work to align policies and strategies that promote development in conflict-affected areas, addressing poverty, unemployment, and infrastructure deficits.

Conflict Transformation

Diplomacy can facilitate peacemaking efforts, as seen in the Sudanese peace agreement, where diplomats played a pivotal role in resolving conflicts and fostering stability. Post-conflict reconstruction is an essential diplomacy effort that helps coordinate international efforts to rebuild infrastructure, institutions, and communities.

Humanitarian Assistance

Diplomacy plays a vital role in negotiating access for humanitarian organizations to deliver aid in conflict zones, addressing immediate needs, and creating conditions for development. Also, diplomats advocate for the adherence to humanitarian principles, such as neutrality and impartiality, ensuring that aid reaches those in need.

Peacebuilding and Reconciliation

Diplomacy provides support for peacebuilding and reconciliation efforts in conflict-affected regions. The involvement of diplomatic envoys and mediators can help bridge divides and facilitate dialogue. Diplomacy builds trust among conflicting parties and communities, which is essential for long-term peace and development.

In summary, diplomacy is critical in addressing violent extremism and promoting development by preventing conflicts, countering extremist ideologies, fostering international cooperation, coordinating development efforts, and facilitating peace and reconciliation. Effective diplomacy is essential for creating the conditions necessary to build peaceful and prosperous societies free from the grip of violent extremism

Theories Relevant to Diplomacy for Conflict Resolution

Realism

Realism emphasizes the pursuit of national interests and the use of power to achieve them. In conflict resolution, realist diplomacy can involve negotiations that seek to secure a nation's interests while avoiding war or further escalation. Diplomats may use power, leverage, and alliances to reach favourable settlements.

Liberalism

Liberal diplomacy promotes values like democracy, human rights, and economic interdependence. It is relevant to conflict resolution through diplomatic efforts to foster cooperation, international institutions, and rule-based negotiations. Liberal diplomats may advocate for peace agreements that promote democracy and human rights.

Constructivism

Constructivism emphasizes the role of ideas, norms, and identities in shaping diplomacy. In conflict resolution, constructivist diplomacy can involve changing perceptions and narratives to create an environment conducive to peace. Diplomats may work to alter the identities and narratives of conflicting parties to facilitate reconciliation.

Game Theory

Game theory provides a framework for analyzing strategic interactions among parties. In conflict resolution, diplomats can use game theory to understand the motivations and incentives of different actors. It can help design negotiation strategies that lead to mutually beneficial outcomes.

Diplomacy of Restraint

The diplomacy of restraint theory suggests that diplomacy can be used to manage and de-escalate conflicts by avoiding provocations and confrontations. This approach is highly relevant to conflict resolution as diplomats aim to prevent conflicts from spiralling out of control and seek to de-escalate existing ones.

Track I, Track II, and Track III Diplomacy

These theories distinguish between official government-led diplomacy (Track I), unofficial diplomatic efforts involving non-state actors (Track II), and citizen-to-citizen diplomacy (Track III). They are relevant to conflict resolution by involving multiple levels of diplomacy and fostering dialogue among various stakeholders, including civil society, to build trust and find common ground.

Diplomacy of Small States

Small states often use diplomatic strategies emphasizing neutrality, mediation, and coalition-building. These approaches can be relevant to conflict resolution by providing impartial mediators and facilitators in international conflicts.

Crisis Diplomacy

Crisis diplomacy deals with the management of acute international crises. It is highly relevant to conflict resolution as it focuses on de-escalation, crisis communication, and negotiation during emergencies to prevent conflicts from erupting into full-blown wars.

Public Diplomacy

Public diplomacy involves engaging with foreign publics and influencing their perceptions and attitudes. Conflict resolution can shape public opinion to support peace efforts and build international support for peaceful solutions.

Soft Power Diplomacy

Soft power diplomacy uses culture, education, and diplomacy to influence others. Conflict resolution can promote reconciliation, understanding, and cooperation among conflicting parties through cultural exchanges, educational programs, and humanitarian initiatives.

These theories of diplomacy provide various lenses through which diplomats and mediators can approach conflict resolution. Depending on the nature of the conflict and the parties involved, diplomats may draw from multiple theories and approaches to find practical solutions and build sustainable peace.

Review Questions

1. What economic factors contribute to violent conflicts in underdeveloped regions?
2. How does social and ethnic diversity interact with underdevelopment to escalate conflicts?
3. What role do inadequate governance and corruption play in perpetuating conflicts in underdeveloped areas?
4. How can diplomacy prevent conflicts from escalating into violent extremism?

Provide examples of external interventions that have exacerbated conflicts in underdeveloped regions.

Discussion Points

1. Discuss the challenges of delivering humanitarian assistance in conflict zones and the role of diplomacy in overcoming these challenges.
2. Explore the impact of resource scarcity on conflicts and the potential for diplomatic solutions to address resource-related disputes.
3. Debate the effectiveness of different diplomatic theories and approaches

in resolving protracted conflicts in regions like Syria and Afghanistan.

4. Analyze the role of diplomacy in fostering regional cooperation to address cross-border extremist threats and promote stability.

5. Discuss the ethical considerations of diplomatic strategies prioritizing national interests versus those prioritizing human rights and democracy promotion in conflict resolution.

CHAPTER THREE: DIPLOMACY'S ROLE IN COUNTERING EXTREMISM AND FOSTERING DEVELOPMENT

Summary of Chapter Three

1. Diplomatic Strategies for Countering Extremism and Promoting Development: Diplomatic strategies are essential for addressing violent extremism (CVE) and promoting development. These strategies include preventive diplomacy, promoting good governance and the rule of law, supporting development, cultural and educational diplomacy, countering radicalization and extremist propaganda, conflict resolution and peacebuilding, community engagement and social cohesion, and humanitarian diplomacy.

2. Examples of Diplomatic Interventions: Case studies demonstrate the effectiveness of diplomatic interventions in resolving conflicts and fostering development. Examples include the Dayton Accords in Bosnia, the Comprehensive Peace Agreement in Sudan, the Good Friday Agreement in Northern Ireland, and diplomatic efforts in Mozambique and Sierra Leone.

3. Diplomatic Approaches to Addressing Violent Extremism and Development: Diplomatic approaches encompass a range of strategies, including preventive diplomacy, counterterrorism diplomacy, multilateral initiatives, building alliances and coalitions, conflict resolution and

peacebuilding, allocating resources and aid, and promoting norms and values.

4. Multilateral Diplomacy and International Cooperation: Multilateral diplomacy and international cooperation are crucial for addressing violent extremism and development. These approaches promote a unified response, sharing of information and best practices, building alliances and coalitions, conflict resolution and peacebuilding, allocating resources and aid, and promoting norms and values.

Diplomatic strategies counter-extremism and development

Diplomatic strategies are pivotal in countering violent extremism (CVE) and promoting development. Diplomacy can be used to address the root causes of extremism, build international partnerships, and foster stability in regions affected by violence. Here are critical diplomatic CVE strategies that serve to promote development as well

Preventive Diplomacy

Conflict Prevention: Diplomats can engage in preventive diplomacy by identifying potential sources of conflict and taking early action to prevent their escalation into violence, which involves using diplomacy to address grievances, promote dialogue, and build trust among conflicting parties.

Mediation and Negotiation: Diplomats can mediate and facilitate negotiations between conflicting groups or states to prevent conflicts and encourage peaceful resolutions.

Promoting Good Governance and Rule of Law

Diplomatic Pressure: Diplomats can use diplomatic pressure and incentives to encourage governments to uphold good governance, the rule of law, and human rights, reducing the potential for grievances that fuel extremism.

Anti-Corruption Efforts: Diplomacy can support international anti-corruption initiatives and encourage governments to combat corruption, which can cause instability and extremism.

Supporting Development Diplomacy

Economic Diplomacy: Diplomacy can secure international investment, foreign aid, and development assistance for conflict-affected regions to help rebuild infrastructure, create jobs, and reduce poverty, addressing critical drivers of extremism.

Development Partnerships: Diplomats can foster development partnerships with countries, organizations, and NGOs to coordinate efforts and maximize the impact of development programs.

Cultural and Educational Diplomacy

Promoting Tolerance and Understanding: Cultural and educational diplomacy initiatives can promote tolerance, understanding, and cultural exchange, countering extremist ideologies that thrive on intolerance and hatred.

Youth Engagement: Diplomacy can support youth engagement programs, scholarships, and exchanges to empower young people with educational opportunities and alternatives to extremism.

Countering Radicalization and Extremist Propaganda

Diplomats can facilitate international cooperation on counterterrorism efforts, including intelligence sharing, law enforcement collaboration, and efforts to combat online extremist propaganda. They can also help secure support and resources for deradicalization and rehabilitation programs to reintegrate former extremists into society.

Conflict Resolution and Peacebuilding

Diplomats can engage in peace negotiations and peacebuilding efforts to resolve conflicts, address grievances, and create the conditions for development in post-conflict societies, and equally support stabilization initiatives in conflict zones, including demobilization and disarmament of combatants, the provision of essential services, and the establishment of governance structures.

Community Engagement and Social Cohesion

Diplomatic Outreach: Diplomats can engage with local communities, religious leaders, and civil society organizations to promote social cohesion and community resilience against extremism.

Interfaith Dialogue: Diplomacy can foster interfaith dialogue and religious tolerance to counter extremist narratives that exploit religious divisions.

Humanitarian Diplomacy

Diplomatic efforts can negotiate access for humanitarian organizations to deliver aid to conflict-affected areas, address immediate needs and build trust within communities, and advocate for the protection of civilians and respect for international humanitarian law in conflict zones.

In summary, diplomatic strategies are indispensable in countering violent extremism and promoting development by addressing the underlying causes of conflict, fostering cooperation, and creating conditions for stability and growth. Effective diplomacy often involves a combination of these strategies tailored to the specific context of each conflict-affected region.

Examples of Diplomatic Interventions

The Dayton Accords - brokered by the United States at the Wright-Patterson Air Force Base in Ohio- ended the war. Diplomats from the U.S., Europe, and Russia were critical in negotiations. The agreement divided Bosnia into two semi-autonomous entities and established a central government. Diplomats worked to rebuild infrastructure, institutions, and governance systems. International support and development aid poured into the region, contributing to post-conflict reconstruction and recovery.

Comprehensive Peace Agreement in Sudan (2005) - The Second Sudanese Civil War (1983-2005) between the Sudanese government and the Sudan People's Liberation Army (SPLA) resulted in widespread displacement and humanitarian crises. Diplomatic efforts led by the Intergovernmental Authority on Development (IGAD) and supported by the U.S. and the African Union culminated in the Comprehensive Peace Agreement (CPA) in Naivasha, Kenya. The CPA ended the civil war, granted South Sudan autonomy, and paved the way for the independence referendum in 2011. Diplomatic engagement continued during South Sudan's nation-building phase, with international support for development and stability.

Good Friday Agreement in Northern Ireland (1998) - Sectarian violence and conflict in Northern Ireland persisted for decades, resulting in substantial loss of life and economic stagnation. The Good Friday Agreement, also known as the Belfast Agreement, was brokered by diplomats from the United Kingdom, Ireland, and the United States. The agreement established a power-sharing government and addressed identity, governance, and justice issues. Diplomatic efforts significantly reduced violence and created an environment conducive to economic development and investment.

Mozambique Peace Agreement (1992) - Mozambique experienced a brutal civil war (1977-1992) between the ruling FRELIMO party and the opposition RENAMO movement. Diplomats from several countries, including the United Nations, Italy, and the United States, facilitated negotiations between the warring parties. The Mozambique Peace Agreement led to a ceasefire, disarmament, and the reintegration of combatants. Diplomatic efforts paved the way for restoring stability, returning refugees, and significant international development assistance, contributing to the country's post-conflict recovery.

Sierra Leone Peace Process (2001) - Sierra Leone endured a brutal civil war (1991-2002) characterized by widespread atrocities, child soldiers, and diamond-related conflict. The Lomé Peace Agreement, brokered by the Economic Community of West African States (ECOWAS), the United Nations, and other international actors, ended the conflict. Diplomatic efforts led to rebel forces' disarmament and child soldiers' reintegration. Subsequent international engagement, including peacekeeping and development assistance, helped rebuild Sierra Leone's institutions and infrastructure.

These case studies illustrate how diplomatic interventions can end violent conflicts and create opportunities for development and peacebuilding. In collaboration with international organizations and stakeholders, diplomacy has played a pivotal role in resolving conflicts, negotiating peace agreements, and facilitating post-conflict reconstruction and development.

Diplomatic Approaches to Addressing Violent Extremism and Development

Generally, diplomatic approaches to addressing violent extremism and promoting development involve a range of strategies and initiatives that leverage diplomacy to mitigate the root causes of extremism and create conditions for sustainable development. Here are several diplomatic approaches to tackle these complex challenges:

Preventive Diplomacy

Early Warning Systems: Diplomats can work to establish and support early warning systems to detect potential conflicts and extremist threats before they escalate.

Conflict Mediation and Prevention: Diplomats can engage with conflicting parties to mediate disputes, address grievances, and negotiate settlements before violence erupts.

Counterterrorism Diplomacy

Diplomacy can facilitate international cooperation on counterterrorism efforts, including intelligence sharing, law enforcement collaboration, and efforts to disrupt terrorist financing networks. Equally, diplomatic initiatives can promote and support deradicalization and rehabilitation programs for individuals involved in extremism, both domestically and internationally.

Multilateral Initiatives

Diplomats can use the United Nations (UN) as a platform to address violent extremism and development issues through resolutions, sanctions, peacekeeping missions, and humanitarian assistance. Equally, regional diplomatic forums, such as the European Union (EU), African Union (AU), or Organization of American States (OAS), can provide platforms for regional cooperation in addressing extremism and fostering development.

Conflict Resolution and Peacebuilding

Diplomatic efforts can lead to peace negotiations and agreements that address the root causes of conflicts, reduce violence, and create an environment conducive to development. Diplomacy can also coordinate international support for post-conflict reconstruction efforts, including rebuilding infrastructure, establishing governance structures, and promoting economic development.

Development Diplomacy

Diplomats can negotiate to secure foreign aid and development assistance for conflict-affected regions, focusing on poverty reduction, job creation, and infrastructure development. Diplomatic missions can promote investment in conflict-affected areas to stimulate economic growth and job opportunities, thereby reducing the appeal of extremist ideologies.

Cultural and Educational Diplomacy

Diplomatic initiatives can foster interfaith dialogue and religious tolerance to counter extremist narratives that exploit religious divisions and facilitate educational and cultural exchanges to promote young people's understanding, tolerance, and critical thinking.

Humanitarian Diplomacy

Diplomats can negotiate with parties to conflicts to ensure safe access for humanitarian organizations to provide aid to affected populations and advocate for the protection of civilians and respect for international humanitarian law in conflict zones.

Youth Engagement

Diplomacy can promote creating entry points and participation spaces to include youth in decision-making processes, community development, and peacebuilding initiatives to prevent their recruitment into extremist groups. Equally, youth empowerment programs can be supported.

These diplomatic approaches are interrelated and often require a combination of efforts to effectively address the complex challenges of violent extremism and promote sustainable development. Diplomats coordinate with governments, international organizations, civil society, and local communities to develop and implement comprehensive strategies to mitigate the drivers of extremism and support development in conflict-affected areas.

Multilateral diplomacy and international cooperation in addressing Extremism and Development

Multilateral diplomacy and international cooperation are essential to addressing violent extremism and development comprehensively and effectively. These approaches involve multiple countries, international organizations, and stakeholders working together to tackle the complex challenges associated with these issues. How multilateral diplomacy and international cooperation play a crucial role in addressing extremism and development is explained below.

Promoting a Unified Response

Violent Extremism: Multilateral diplomacy allows countries to develop a unified response to counterterrorism and counter violent extremism (CVE). International cooperation ensures that all nations can coordinate efforts to prevent the spread of extremist ideologies and combat extremist groups.

Development: Multilateral development initiatives, such as the Sustainable Development Goals (SDGs) adopted by the United Nations, provide a common framework for countries to work together in addressing issues like poverty, inequality, and lack of access to education and healthcare. Collaboration among countries is essential to achieving these global development goals.

Sharing Information and Best Practices

Violent Extremism: International cooperation facilitates sharing intelligence, information, and best practices in countering extremist threats. Countries can learn from one another's experiences and develop more effective strategies to combat radicalization and terrorism.

Development: Multilateral platforms enable countries to exchange knowledge and successful development strategies. Learning from each other's experiences can lead to more efficient and targeted development efforts.

Building Alliances and Coalitions

Violent Extremism: Multilateral diplomacy allows countries to build alliances and coalitions to address specific extremist threats. For example, the Global Coalition to Defeat ISIS is a multilateral effort involving over 80 countries working to defeat the Islamic State terrorist group.

Development: Countries can form alliances and partnerships to pool resources, expertise, and funding to support development initiatives in conflict-affected regions. For instance, the African Union's New Partnership for Africa's Development (NEPAD) promotes collaboration among African countries to achieve sustainable development.

Conflict Resolution and Peacebuilding

Violent Extremism: Multilateral diplomacy plays a crucial role in mediating conflicts that contribute to the rise of violent extremism. Diplomatic efforts, often led by international organizations like the United Nations, aim to resolve conflicts and create conditions for peace and stability.

Development: Peace is a prerequisite for development. Multilateral diplomacy supports peacebuilding and post-conflict reconstruction, ensuring that development efforts can be effectively implemented in conflict-affected areas.

Allocating Resources and Aid

Violent Extremism: Multilateral cooperation helps countries pool resources and coordinate international aid for counterterrorism and CVE efforts, including funding programs to address the underlying drivers of extremism, such as poverty and lack of education.

Development: Multilateral organizations and donor countries allocate financial resources for development projects, humanitarian aid, and capacity-building programs in conflict-affected regions. International cooperation ensures that aid is directed to where it is needed most.

Promoting Norms and Values

Violent Extremism: Multilateral diplomacy reinforces international norms against terrorism and violent extremism. Countries come together to condemn acts of terrorism and commit to upholding human rights and the rule of law.

Development: Multilateral initiatives promote shared values related to human rights, gender equality, and sustainable development. They help hold countries accountable for meeting these standards and commitments.

In summary, multilateral diplomacy and international cooperation are vital in addressing violent extremism and development challenges. These approaches foster collaboration, enhance the effectiveness of efforts, and promote a unified response to complex global issues. By working together, countries and international organizations can make significant progress in preventing extremism and promoting sustainable development in conflict-affected areas.

Review Questions

1. What are the critical diplomatic strategies for preventing conflicts from escalating into violence and extremism?
2. How does diplomacy promote good governance and the rule of law in conflict-affected regions?
3. Explain the role of cultural and educational diplomacy in countering

extremist ideologies.

4. How can diplomats effectively engage in conflict resolution and peacebuilding efforts?

5. What are the benefits of multilateral diplomacy and international cooperation in addressing extremism and development challenges?

Discussion Points

1. Discuss the challenges of implementing preventive diplomacy in regions with entrenched conflicts and extremist ideologies. What are the limitations of this approach?

2. Explore the ethical considerations of diplomatic engagements with governments that may have poor human rights records but are crucial for counterterrorism efforts.

3. Analyze the role of cultural diplomacy in promoting tolerance and understanding among diverse communities and countering extremist narratives.

4. Debate the effectiveness of international sanctions as a diplomatic tool in countering extremism and encouraging good governance.

5. Discuss the importance of involving civil society organizations and local communities in diplomatic efforts to promote social cohesion and resilience against extremism.

CHAPTER FOUR: DIPLOMACY'S COMPLEX PATHWAYS TO DEVELOPMENT AND SECURITY

Summary of Chapter Four

1. Bilateral Diplomacy and Partnerships for Development and Security: Bilateral diplomacy and partnerships play a crucial role in international relations, facilitating collaboration on development and security. They involve foreign aid and assistance, capacity building, trade and investment promotion, military alliances, counterterrorism cooperation, peacekeeping, diplomatic relations, crisis management, joint research and innovation, and people-to-people diplomacy.

2. Track II Diplomacy and Dialogue for Conflict Resolution and Development: Track II diplomacy and dialogue involve non-governmental actors and provide unofficial channels for communication and negotiation. They facilitate communication and trust-building, explore creative solutions, implement confidence-building measures, prepare the ground for official diplomacy, promote inclusivity, encourage regional cooperation, prevent crises, and foster people-to-people relations.

3. Economic Diplomacy, Counter-Extremism, and Sustainable Development: Economic diplomacy leverages economic resources and policies to promote national interests, economic growth, and development.

It includes trade and investment promotion, development assistance, aid coordination, economic cooperation, negotiation of agreements, economic governance and reform, alignment with Sustainable Development Goals (SDGs), and public-private partnerships (PPPs).

4. Challenges/Limitations of Diplomacy in Addressing Violent Extremism and Development: Diplomacy faces several challenges and limitations in addressing violent extremism and development, including lack of trust and credibility, geopolitical rivalries, resistance from extremist groups, limited access to conflict zones, incomplete information, resistance to change, slow processes, limited enforcement mechanisms, resource constraints, political transitions, cultural and linguistic barriers, external interference, public opinion, and short-term vs long-term goals.

Bilateral diplomacy and partnerships for development and security

Bilateral diplomacy and partnerships are essential components of international relations, enabling countries to work together to achieve common goals, including development and security. Bilateral diplomacy refers to the diplomatic relations and interactions between two countries, while partnerships can involve bilateral cooperation or collaboration with multiple countries. How bilateralism and partnerships contribute to development and security are explained in detail below:

Development Partnerships

Foreign Aid and Assistance: Bilateral diplomacy allows countries to provide foreign aid, development assistance, and technical expertise to support partner nations' economic and social development. Donor countries often establish development partnerships to address poverty reduction, healthcare, education, and infrastructure development in recipient countries.

Capacity Building: Bilateral partnerships facilitate capacity-building programs in which donor countries help strengthen partner countries' institutional and human resource capacities, often the poorer or violence-stricken countries. This support can enhance governance, improve public services, and promote sustainable development.

Trade and Investment: Bilateral trade agreements and investment partnerships can stimulate economic growth and development in both countries. These partnerships can create jobs and drive economic development by facilitating the flow of goods, services, and investments.

Security Partnerships

Military Alliances: Bilateral military alliances and defence partnerships are established to enhance national and regional security. Countries often engage in defence pacts and mutual agreements to deter potential adversaries and collectively respond to security threats.

Counterterrorism Cooperation: Bilateral security partnerships focus on countering terrorism and transnational threats. Countries share intelligence, conduct joint operations, and coordinate law enforcement efforts to combat terrorism and extremist activities.

Peacekeeping and Conflict Resolution: Bilateral diplomacy is crucial for mediating conflicts and peacekeeping operations. Countries may partner to deploy peacekeeping troops or negotiate to resolve conflicts and prevent further violence.

Diplomatic Relations and Communication

Diplomatic Channels: Bilateral diplomacy is the primary means for countries to establish and maintain diplomatic relations. Through embassies, consulates, and diplomatic missions, countries communicate and cooperate on various issues, including development and security.

Crisis Management: Bilateral diplomacy enables countries to address crises and conflicts directly. Diplomatic communication is vital in diffusing tensions, de-escalating conflicts, and finding diplomatic solutions to security challenges.

Joint Research and Innovation

Countries engage in bilateral partnerships for joint research, innovation, and technology transfer. Such collaborations can lead to advancements in various fields, including healthcare, agriculture, and renewable energy, contributing to development.

Regional and Global Influence

Bilateral partnerships contribute to regional stability by fostering cooperation among neighbouring countries. Stable regions are more conducive to development, trade, and investment. At the same time, bilateral partnerships cause countries to build numerous bilateral relationships that, across the board, culminate in better international organizations and global governance structures. By working together, they can address global challenges, such as climate change and pandemics, with both development and security implications.

Cultural and Educational Exchanges

People-to-People Diplomacy: Bilateral partnerships can promote people-to-people diplomacy through cultural exchanges, scholarships, and educational programs that promote understanding, tolerance, and cooperation among citizens. These initiatives can promote peace and development by fostering cross-cultural dialogue and relationships.

In summary, bilateral diplomacy and partnerships are vital tools for countries to address complex challenges related to development and security. These diplomatic efforts facilitate collaboration, resource-sharing, and problem-solving on bilateral and multilateral levels, ultimately contributing to the well-being and stability of nations and regions.

Track II Diplomacy and Dialogue for Conflict Resolution and Development

Track II diplomacy and dialogue play significant roles in conflict resolution and development by providing unofficial channels for communication, negotiation, and problem-solving. These processes involve non-governmental actors, such as civil society organizations, academics, and individuals, who can often engage more informally and flexibly than official state representatives. Here is how Track II diplomacy and dialogue contribute to conflict resolution and development:

Facilitating Communication and Trust-Building

Track II diplomacy allows conflicting parties to communicate indirectly and build trust. Neutral mediators and facilitators can encourage dialogue, even when official diplomatic channels are strained or non-existent. In post-conflict situations, Track II dialogue can foster trust and cooperation among communities, local leaders, and development organizations, helping to create an environment conducive to development initiatives.

Exploring Creative Solutions

Track II dialogue allows for brainstorming and exploration of unconventional solutions to complex conflicts. Participants often bring fresh perspectives and innovative ideas that may be unrestricted by official policies. In addressing development challenges, Track II initiatives can promote innovative approaches and explore unconventional solutions that may not be readily considered within traditional development frameworks.

Confidence-Building Measures

Track II diplomacy can help establish and implement confidence-building measures (CBMs) that reduce tension and prevent conflicts from escalating. These measures can include ceasefire agreements, humanitarian access, and prisoner exchanges. CBMs can create an environment of security and stability conducive to development efforts, reducing the risk of violence and disruption of development projects.

Preparing Ground for Official Diplomacy

Track II dialogues can lay the groundwork for official diplomatic negotiations by identifying common ground, areas of disagreement, and potential solutions. This preparation can facilitate more productive official negotiations. In post-conflict situations, Track II dialogues help build consensus and create a shared vision for development priorities, which official development agencies can endorse and support.

Inclusive Peace Processes

Track II diplomacy often involves a broader range of stakeholders, including marginalized groups, civil society organizations, and local communities. This inclusivity contributes to more comprehensive and sustainable peace processes. Inclusive Track II dialogues can ensure that development planning considers the needs and aspirations of all segments of society, reducing the risk of exclusion and resentment.

Regional and Cross-Border Cooperation

Track II dialogues can facilitate regional and cross-border cooperation to address shared security concerns and conflicts that spill over national borders. Regional cooperation can promote economic integration, trade, and infrastructure development, fostering regional stability and development.

Crisis Prevention and Management

Track II dialogue can serve as an early warning mechanism, helping to identify and address emerging conflicts before they escalate into violence. By preventing conflicts and crises, Track II initiatives contribute to an environment where development efforts can be implemented more effectively and with fewer interruptions.

Promoting People-to-People Relations

Track II dialogues often involve individuals from diverse backgrounds, promoting people-to-people relations and breaking down stereotypes and prejudices that may fuel conflicts. Improved social cohesion and understanding among communities contribute to a more stable and supportive environment for development initiatives.

In summary, Track II diplomacy and dialogue complement official diplomacy in conflict resolution and development efforts. They provide valuable opportunities for diverse actors to engage in peacebuilding, foster trust, explore innovative solutions, and ensure that the perspectives and needs of all stakeholders are considered. By promoting dialogue and cooperation at multiple levels of society, Track II initiatives contribute to more comprehensive and sustainable solutions to complex challenges.

Economic Diplomacy, Counter-Extremism, and Sustainable development

Economic diplomacy leverages a country's economic resources, trade relations, and policies to advance its national interests and promote economic growth and development. When used effectively, economic diplomacy can play a significant role in promoting inclusive and sustainable development. Here are critical aspects of economic diplomacy and how it contributes to counter-extremism and sustainable development.

Trade and Investment Promotion

Market Access: Economic diplomacy aims to negotiate favourable trade agreements that provide businesses with better market access. By expanding export opportunities, countries can generate economic growth and create jobs, contributing to inclusive development.

Foreign Direct Investment (FDI): Economic diplomacy attracts foreign investment by creating a favourable climate. FDI can stimulate economic development by infusing capital, technology, and expertise into the host country's economy.

Development Assistance and Aid Coordination

Official Development Assistance (ODA): Economic diplomacy plays a role in securing development assistance and aid from donor countries and international organizations. Effective diplomacy can ensure that aid is directed toward priority areas, such as education, healthcare, and infrastructure.

Aid Coordination: Diplomats can facilitate coordination among various donors to prevent duplication of efforts, enhance aid effectiveness, and promote sustainable development projects.

Economic Cooperation and Regional Integration

Regional Trade Agreements: Economic diplomacy supports the negotiation of regional trade agreements, which can promote economic integration, increase trade, and stimulate economic growth within a region.

Infrastructure Development: Diplomacy can facilitate cross-border infrastructure projects, such as transportation and energy networks, which can boost regional connectivity and economic development.

Negotiation of Bilateral and Multilateral Agreements

Intellectual Property Rights (IPR) Protection: Economic diplomacy can lead to agreements on IPR protection, which encourages innovation and technology transfer, contributing to long-term economic development.

Environmental Agreements: Diplomacy is essential for negotiating international environmental protection and sustainable development agreements, such as climate change accords.

Economic Governance and Reform

Policy Advocacy: Economic diplomacy can include advocating for economic policy reforms that create an enabling environment for business growth, entrepreneurship, and job creation.

Good Governance: Diplomats can engage with host countries to promote transparency, anti-corruption measures, and good governance practices crucial for sustainable development.

Promoting Inclusive Growth

Diplomacy can advocate for fair trade policies prioritizing inclusive growth, fair labour practices, and protecting vulnerable groups. They can also facilitate international cooperation to develop social safety nets and support systems that help mitigate the negative impacts of economic changes on marginalized communities.

Sustainable Development Goals (SDGs)

Diplomats can work to align national economic policies and development strategies with the United Nations Sustainable Development Goals (SDGs) to ensure that economic diplomacy efforts contribute to broader global development objectives.

Public-Private Partnerships (PPPs)

Diplomacy can encourage collaboration between governments and the private sector to finance and implement development projects. PPPs can leverage private-sector resources and expertise for infrastructure development and service delivery.

In summary, economic diplomacy is critical for promoting inclusive and sustainable development. By leveraging economic resources, trade relations, and economic policies, countries can generate economic growth, reduce poverty, and create opportunities for all segments of society. Effective economic diplomacy involves strategic negotiations, partnerships, and policy advocacy to align economic objectives with development goals, contributing to a more equitable and sustainable future.

Challenges/Limitations of Diplomacy in Addressing Violent Extremism and Development

Diplomacy plays a crucial role in addressing violent extremism and promoting development, but it also faces several challenges and limitations in these complex endeavours. Understanding these challenges is essential for developing more effective diplomatic strategies. Here are some of the key challenges and limitations:

Lack of Trust and Credibility: Deep-seated distrust among the conflicting parties makes resolving some conflicts more challenging. Diplomats prioritize trust building.

Geopolitical Rivalries: States, incredibly advanced countries, tend to prioritize their geopolitical interests over conflict resolution and development in certain regions, which can hinder diplomatic efforts.

Extremist Groups: Violent extremist groups often operate outside the realm of diplomacy and may not be amenable to negotiations or agreements, making engaging with them through pugh traditional diplomatic channels challenging.

Limited Access to Conflict Zones: Often during conflict, diplomats become targets, making secure access to conflict-affected areas difficult, which impedes their ability to assess the situation on the ground and engage directly with local actors. Equally, diplomats may have limited influence over non-state actors involved in extremism and conflict.

Incomplete Information: The conflict situation and dynamics are often too complex to understand and act appropriately.

Resistance to Change: In some cases, governments and power structures may resist diplomatic pressure for reforms that could address the root causes of extremism, such as corruption and authoritarianism.

Slow Diplomatic Processes: Diplomatic negotiations are sometimes too lengthy and time-consuming, especially when multiple parties are involved. Prolonged negotiations can lead to continued violence and suffering.

Limited Enforcement Mechanisms: Diplomatic agreements may need more effective enforcement mechanisms, making it challenging to ensure that parties adhere to their commitments.

Resource Constraints: Diplomatic missions may need more resources, both human and financial, which can restrict their ability to engage comprehensively in conflict resolution and development efforts.

Political Transitions: Political instability, regime changes, or leadership turnover in conflict-affected countries can disrupt ongoing diplomatic efforts and necessitate starting negotiations anew.

Cultural and Linguistic Barriers: Diplomats may face challenges related to cultural and linguistic differences, which can hinder effective communication and understanding among parties.

External Interference: External actors, including neighbouring countries, may interfere in conflict and development processes, further complicating diplomatic efforts.

Public Opinion: In democratic countries, public opinion and political pressures can influence diplomatic decisions, sometimes leading to suboptimal outcomes in conflict resolution and development.

Short-Term vs. Long-Term Goals: Diplomatic efforts may focus more on short-term stability and immediate crisis management rather than addressing the long-term structural factors that fuel extremism and hinder development.

Despite these challenges and limitations, diplomacy remains the most sustainable tool in addressing violent extremism and promoting development. Diplomats must adapt to changing circumstances, engage in creative and flexible approaches, and work with other stakeholders, including international organizations, civil society, and local communities, to overcome these obstacles and advance peace and development.

Review Questions

1. How does bilateral diplomacy contribute to both development and security goals?
2. What are the critical roles of Track II diplomacy and dialogue in conflict resolution and development?
3. How can economic diplomacy promote sustainable development and counter-extremism?
4. What are some significant challenges and limitations diplomats face in addressing violent extremism and development?
5. How can public opinion influence diplomatic conflict resolution and development decisions?

Discussion Points

1. Discuss the role of bilateral military alliances in enhancing national and regional security. What are the advantages and disadvantages of such alliances?
2. Explore the potential benefits of economic diplomacy in promoting sustainable development, especially in low-income countries.
3. Analyze the importance of inclusivity in Track II diplomacy and how it contributes to more comprehensive peace processes.
4. Debate the ethical considerations of engaging in economic partnerships with countries with poor human rights records.

5. Discuss how the challenges and limitations of diplomacy can be addressed or mitigated to improve its effectiveness in promoting development and security.

CHAPTER FIVE: MULTILATERAL DIPLOMACY IN TACKLING EXTREMISM AND DEVELOPMENT CHALLENGES

Multilateral Diplomacy and Challenging Trust-Building Among Nations

The lack of trust and cooperation among nations hinders efforts to address violent extremism and development challenges. Suspicion, historical grievances, and conflicting interests can create barriers to effective diplomatic engagement. Below are notable examples to illustrate these challenges.

Israel-Palestine Conflict

The perennial Israel-Palestine conflict is marked by deep-seated mistrust between the two sides and falling back to extremist religious narratives. Decades of violence, territorial disputes, and failed peace talks have eroded trust in the possibility of a negotiated settlement. Despite numerous attempts at diplomacy and multiple peace initiatives, the conflict continues to fester. Parties on both sides often accuse each other of bad faith, making it difficult to reach a sustainable resolution.

India-Pakistan Relations

India and Pakistan have a long history of conflicts and mistrust, including wars and ongoing disputes over Kashmir. Terrorist attacks and allegations of state-sponsored terrorism have further strained relations. Diplomatic efforts to normalize relations and address shared challenges like poverty and extremism are often hampered by political tensions, making it challenging for the two countries to cooperate effectively.

North Korea's Nuclear Program

North Korea's pursuit of nuclear weapons has been a significant international concern. Years of negotiations, agreements, and subsequent violations have eroded trust between North Korea and countries like the United States. Despite several diplomatic engagements, including the Six-Party Talks, progress on denuclearization has been slow due to a lack of trust and North Korea's reluctance to give up its nuclear capabilities.

Syria Civil War

The Syrian conflict has involved multiple international actors, including the Syrian government, rebel groups, Russia, the United States, and others. These parties have conflicting interests and have accused each other of supporting extremism. Attempts to negotiate a political solution have been complicated by distrust among the parties, leading to prolonged violence and suffering in the region.

Climate Change Negotiations

International climate change negotiations often need help due to distrust among nations. Developed countries may question the commitments of developing nations, while developing nations may see developed nations as not doing enough to address climate change. Progress in climate negotiations can be slow as countries grapple with trust, equity, and shared responsibility issues, which have implications for sustainable development, as climate change affects vulnerable regions disproportionately.

Western Sahara Conflict

The Western Sahara conflict between Morocco and the Polisario Front has persisted for decades, marked by mistrust and competing claims to the territory. Despite diplomatic efforts by the United Nations, a lasting solution remains elusive due to the lack of trust between the parties and the difficulty of finding a compromise.

In the abovementioned cases, the lack of trust and cooperation among nations has impeded diplomatic efforts to address violent extremism and development challenges. Rebuilding trust and fostering cooperation often requires sustained dialogue, confidence-building measures, and a commitment to addressing conflicts' underlying grievances and root causes. These challenges underscore the importance of diplomacy in bridging divides and finding common ground, even in the face of profoundly entrenched mistrust.

Balancing Security Concerns and Human Rights in Diplomacy

Balancing security concerns and human rights in diplomatic efforts is complex and often delicate. Governments must address security threats while upholding fundamental human rights principles. Striking the right balance between these two priorities is essential to ensuring national and international stability. Here are key considerations and examples illustrating this challenge:

Necessity and Proportionality

Diplomatic efforts should ensure that security measures, such as surveillance, detention, or counterterrorism operations, are necessary and proportionate to the threat. For example, the U.S. initiated the War on Terror after the September 11 attacks, raising concerns about balancing national security with human rights. Critics argued that some measures, such as the Guantanamo Bay detention facility and mass surveillance programs, were disproportionate and violated human rights.

Rule of Law and Due Process

Diplomatic efforts should ensure that individuals accused of security-related offences have access to legal processes, including fair trials, legal representation, and protection against arbitrary detention. The European Court of Human Rights has ruled against countries that have violated the right to a fair trial in terrorism-related cases, reflecting the importance of upholding due process even in security contexts.

Transparency and Accountability

Diplomatic efforts should encourage transparency in security measures and mechanisms to hold security agencies accountable for abuses. The Snowden revelations about mass surveillance by intelligence agencies raised concerns about a lack of transparency and oversight. Diplomatic discussions ensued, with some countries pushing for greater transparency in intelligence activities.

Protection of Vulnerable Groups

Diplomatic efforts should prioritize the protection of vulnerable groups, such as refugees, migrants, and minority populations, who may face discrimination or abuse in the name of security. Treating refugees and migrants has been a diplomatic challenge in various regions. Balancing security concerns with the rights of displaced populations requires international cooperation and negotiations.

International Humanitarian Law

Diplomatic efforts should ensure compliance with international humanitarian law during armed conflicts, including protecting civilians and humanitarian workers. The conflict in Yemen has raised concerns about violations of international humanitarian law. Diplomatic initiatives, such as peace talks and negotiations, aim to address these concerns while pursuing a resolution to the conflict.

Countering Violent Extremism (CVE)

Diplomatic efforts should include CVE strategies focusing on prevention, addressing root causes, and promoting deradicalization and rehabilitation rather than solely punitive measures. Various countries have developed CVE programs incorporating diplomacy, education, and community engagement to address the ideological drivers of extremism while respecting human rights.

Balancing National and International Interests

Diplomatic efforts should consider national security concerns and international human rights obligations. Striking a proper balance would require negotiations and compromises. Diplomatic discussions within the United Nations often revolve around balancing national sovereignty and international human rights standards. This tension can be seen in debates over interventions in conflicts where human rights abuses occur.

Balancing security concerns and human rights in diplomatic efforts requires careful consideration, dialogue, and negotiation. While security is a legitimate concern for states, it should not come at the expense of fundamental human rights. Diplomacy is crucial for addressing these challenges, promoting dialogue, and seeking solutions to safeguard security and human rights.

Overcoming Political and Ideological Barriers to Diplomacy in Promoting Development

Overcoming political and ideological barriers to diplomacy in promoting development is a complex task that involves navigating differences in values, ideologies, and political interests. Diplomatic efforts aimed at development must address these barriers to foster cooperation and achieve sustainable progress. Here are some strategies and considerations for overcoming political and ideological barriers to diplomacy in promoting development.

Finding Common Ground

Diplomacy should seek common objectives and areas of agreement among parties with divergent political and ideological stances. For example, in climate change negotiations, countries with varying political ideologies and economic interests can find common ground in their commitment to mitigating the impacts of climate change.

Promoting Inclusive Diplomacy

Diplomatic efforts should include diverse stakeholders, including civil society, local communities, and marginalized groups, to ensure a broad spectrum of perspectives and interests are represented. For example, in post-conflict reconstruction, involving local communities in decision-making can help overcome political barriers by fostering inclusivity and ownership of development initiatives.

Building Trust through Dialogue

Diplomatic efforts should prioritize open and sustained dialogue among parties with conflicting ideologies to build trust and foster understanding. The peace process in Northern Ireland included dialogue between conflicting political and ideological groups, leading to the Good Friday Agreement.

Highlighting Interdependence

Diplomacy should emphasize how interdependence among nations necessitates cooperation for mutual benefit, particularly in addressing global challenges. The international response to the COVID-19 pandemic highlighted the interdependence of countries in addressing health crises, driving global cooperation.

Addressing Root Causes

Diplomacy should address the root causes of conflicts and development challenges, including political and ideological grievances. In peace negotiations, addressing underlying political grievances, such as equitable representation and power-sharing, can contribute to lasting peace.

Using Multilateral Platforms

Diplomatic efforts can leverage multilateral organizations and forums to depoliticize development issues and promote consensus. The United Nations and regional organizations often serve as platforms for countries with diverse political ideologies to collaborate on development goals.

Bridging Divides through Track II Diplomacy

Track II diplomacy, involving non-governmental actors, can provide an informal space for individuals with differing political ideologies to engage in dialogue. The Oslo Accords in the Middle East involved informal negotiations led by non-governmental actors, contributing to a breakthrough in the peace process.

Focusing on Pragmatism

Diplomacy should prioritize practical, evidence-based solutions over ideological positions when addressing development challenges. In addressing economic crises, countries may set aside ideological differences to adopt pragmatic economic policies for stability and growth.

Balancing Sovereignty and International Cooperation

Diplomatic efforts should acknowledge the importance of national sovereignty while promoting international cooperation to address global challenges. For example, countries balance sovereignty concerns with international obligations to reduce arms proliferation in disarmament negotiations.

Long-term Engagement

Diplomatic efforts should recognize that overcoming political and ideological barriers may require long-term engagement and commitment to achieve development goals. Sustainable development initiatives often require ongoing diplomacy to navigate political shifts and evolving ideological landscapes.

Overcoming political and ideological barriers to diplomacy in promoting development is an ongoing process that requires patience, persistence, and creative problem-solving. Diplomatic efforts should emphasize cooperation, inclusivity, and a focus on shared interests and values, even in the face of ideological differences, to achieve sustainable development outcomes.

Addressing the Root Causes of Violent Extremism and Underdevelopment

Diplomatic efforts can be pivotal in identifying, understanding, and addressing these complex challenges. How diplomacy can address the root causes of violent extremism and underdevelopment is explained below.

Political Solutions and Conflict Resolution

Diplomacy should focus on resolving conflicts and political disputes contributing to violent extremism and underdevelopment. For example, diplomatic negotiations, such as the Dayton Agreement in Bosnia and Herzegovina, have helped end violent conflicts and create conditions for development.

Inclusivity and Governance

Diplomacy should promote inclusive governance, good governance practices, and respect for human rights to address root causes. For example, diplomatic pressure on governments to ensure inclusive governance and protect minority rights can mitigate grievances that fuel extremism and hinder development.

Economic Development and Poverty Alleviation

Diplomacy can facilitate international partnerships and agreements that promote economic development and poverty reduction in underdeveloped regions. The United Nations Sustainable Development Goals (SDGs) serve as a diplomatic framework for addressing poverty and inequality, which can contribute to extremism.

Education and Counter-Radicalization Efforts

Diplomacy can support educational initiatives and counter-radicalization programs that provide alternative narratives and opportunities for individuals vulnerable to extremism. For instance, diplomatic efforts can involve countries cooperating to develop and fund educational programs to promote tolerance, critical thinking, and resilience against extremist ideologies.

Humanitarian Assistance and Refugee Management

Diplomacy should address humanitarian crises and the displacement of populations, often linked to both extremism and underdevelopment. For example, diplomatic negotiations and cooperation among countries are essential for providing humanitarian aid, protecting refugees, and finding durable solutions to displacement.

Addressing Social and Cultural Factors

Diplomacy should acknowledge the social and cultural dimensions contributing to extremism and underdevelopment and engage with local communities and religious leaders to address them. Diplomatic efforts can facilitate dialogues between religious leaders, community leaders, and governments to counter extremist narratives and promote social cohesion.

Countering Corruption and Inequality

Diplomacy can promote transparency, anti-corruption measures, and policies that reduce income inequality and promote social justice. Diplomatic pressure and international agreements can encourage governments to combat corruption, allocate resources more equitably, and address inequality-related grievances.

Multilateral Cooperation

Diplomacy should encourage multilateral cooperation and partnerships among countries, international organizations, and civil society to address the root causes of extremism and underdevelopment. Initiatives like the Global Counterterrorism Forum (GCTF) bring together countries to share best practices and coordinate efforts to counter extremism diplomatically.

Conflict Prevention

Diplomacy can focus on early warning systems, conflict prevention, and peacebuilding to address the root causes of extremism before they escalate into violence. Diplomatic efforts in conflict-prone regions may include preventive diplomacy, confidence-building measures, and support for mediation and reconciliation.

In summary, diplomacy is crucial for addressing the root causes of violent extremism and underdevelopment. It requires a comprehensive, long-term approach emphasising political solutions, good governance, economic development, education, and local, regional, and international cooperation. By addressing these root causes, diplomacy can contribute to a more stable, secure, and prosperous world.

Review Questions

1. How does the lack of trust among nations impact the resolution of the Israel-Palestine conflict?
2. What are the critical considerations in balancing security concerns and human rights in diplomacy?
3. How can inclusivity and dialogue help overcome political and ideological barriers to diplomacy in promoting development?
4. What are the root causes of violent extremism, and how can diplomacy address them effectively?
5. Why is long-term engagement essential in diplomacy to address development challenges and extremism?

Discussion Points

1. Discuss the role of diplomacy in breaking the cycle of mistrust and hostility between India and Pakistan, particularly in the context of the Kashmir dispute.
2. Explore diplomats' ethical dilemmas when balancing security concerns and human rights, using examples like Guantanamo Bay and mass surveillance.
3. Debate the effectiveness of multilateral diplomacy in addressing global challenges like climate change and how trust issues among nations can hinder progress.
4. Examine the potential impact of grassroots movements and civil society engagement in overcoming political and ideological barriers to diplomacy for development.
5. Discuss the role of diplomacy in promoting inclusive governance and addressing political grievances in conflict-prone regions, such as in post-conflict reconstruction.

CHAPTER SIX: FUTURE OF USING DIPLOMACY TO ADDRESS EXTREMISM AND DEVELOPMENT CHALLENGES

Summary of Chapter Six

1. Evolving Diplomatic Trends: Diplomacy has to evolve to address the challenges posed by extremism and development effectively. Innovative trends such as digital diplomacy, preventive diplomacy, and gender mainstreaming are discussed, and the need for a multidimensional and adaptive approach is emphasized.

2. Digital Diplomacy's Growing Role: Technology, mainly digital diplomacy, is a potent tool for countering extremist propaganda, enhancing governance and transparency, and fostering cultural exchanges. The text underscores the transformative impact of digital tools in diplomacy's engagement and crisis response efforts.

3. Tackling Emerging Challenges: Policymakers must grapple with various challenges, including online radicalization, climate change, refugee crises, and youth engagement. Recognizing these evolving dynamics is crucial for crafting responsive diplomatic strategies.

4. Science Diplomacy and Beyond: The chapter introduces various innovative diplomatic approaches, such as science diplomacy, preventive

diplomacy, vaccine diplomacy, and gender diplomacy. These evolving strategies facilitate engagement and cooperation in the increasingly complex landscape of extremism and development.

5. Multifaceted Financing Models: Diplomacy now requires innovative financing models to address extremism and development effectively. These models aim to mobilize resources efficiently while ensuring investments are directed toward sustainable and peacebuilding initiatives.

6. Preventing Extremism at Its Roots: One of the central themes is the proactive role diplomacy plays in preventing extremism. From political solutions and conflict resolution to addressing the root causes of extremism through social and cultural factors, the chapter underscores the significance of diplomatic efforts in fostering peace and development.

The Future of Diplomacy in Addressing Violent Extremism and Development

To effectively counter violent extremism and support development, diplomacy has to evolve in response to changing global dynamics, emerging threats, and new opportunities. Below are some key trends and considerations for the future of diplomacy in this context:

Integrated Approaches

Diplomacy will increasingly adopt holistic and integrated strategies recognizing the interconnectedness of violent extremism and development. Future efforts will seek to address both issues simultaneously rather than in isolation. Integrated approaches will involve a whole-of-government approach, coordinating various agencies and stakeholders, including civil society, private sector, and international organizations, to pool resources and expertise.

Digital Diplomacy and Technology

Cyber diplomacy is emerging as an essential sub-field. Diplomacy will grapple with the challenges of cyberspace, where extremism often thrives. Digital diplomacy will play a role in countering extremist propaganda and facilitating online counter-narratives. Closely linked to this is the need to embrace Big data and analytics. Diplomatic efforts will increasingly leverage big data and analytics to understand trends, identify early warning signs, and develop evidence-based policies.

Preventive Diplomacy

Early warning systems are now critical. Diplomats prioritize early warning systems and preventive measures to address the root causes of extremism before they escalate into violence. It is more helpful to focus more on conflict prevention, mediation, and peacebuilding to reduce the conditions conducive to violent extremism.

Multilateral Cooperation

Strengthening multilateralism is more important now than ever. Diplomacy will emphasize the importance of international cooperation and the role of multilateral organizations, such as the United Nations, in addressing global challenges. Also, regional organizations and initiatives will become increasingly important in addressing localized drivers of extremism and development issues.

Community and Civil Society Engagement

Diplomacy will prioritize engagement with local communities and civil society organizations as critical partners in countering extremism and promoting development. Countering Violent Extremism (CVE) programs will continue to involve civil society actors in creating tailored interventions and rehabilitation efforts.

Gender Mainstreaming

Diplomatic efforts must fully integrate a gender perspective, recognizing the role of gender dynamics in both violent extremism and development, including the participation of women in peace and security processes.

Climate Change and Environmental Diplomacy

Diplomacy will increasingly address environmental and climate-related drivers of extremism and development challenges, as climate change can exacerbate vulnerabilities and conflicts. Promoting sustainable resource management and equitable access to natural resources as part of development strategies is now more critical.

Soft Power and Cultural Diplomacy

Diplomacy will continue to promote democratic values, human rights, and cultural exchanges to counter extremist ideologies. People-to-people diplomacy and cultural exchanges must be prioritized for improved trust-building and understanding among nations and communities.

Innovative Financing Models

Diplomacy will explore innovative financing models, such as impact investing and public-private partnerships, to mobilize resources for development projects.

Prevention of Violent Extremism in Prisons

Diplomatic efforts will focus on prison rehabilitation programs to prevent the radicalization of inmates and their reintegration into society upon release.

The future of diplomacy in addressing violent extremism and development will require adaptability, collaboration, and a commitment to addressing the root causes of these challenges. It will involve a combination of traditional diplomatic approaches and innovative, technology-driven solutions to navigate an ever-changing global landscape. Ultimately, diplomacy will continue to be an indispensable tool for promoting peace, security, and sustainable development in the 21st century.

Emerging Trends and Challenges in Addressing Extremism and Development

Policymakers and practitioners must stay informed and adapt their strategies to respond to these challenges effectively. Here are some emerging trends and challenges in addressing extremism and development.

Online Radicalization and Cyber Threats

Extremist groups increasingly use the internet to recruit, radicalize, and coordinate activities. Cyber threats pose risks to both security and development efforts. For example, the rise of ISIS propaganda and recruitment efforts on social media platforms is a prominent case. Governments and tech companies have struggled to counter this online presence effectively.

Disinformation and Misinformation

The dominant trend is growing disinformation/misinformation. Disinformation campaigns can exacerbate existing grievances and contribute to radicalization. Distinguishing between genuine information and false narratives is challenging. For example, during the Rohingya crisis, disinformation campaigns fueled tensions and violence in Myanmar, making it challenging to address the underlying issues.

Climate Change and Resource Scarcity

Climate change and resource scarcity are increasingly linked to conflicts and extremism as they contribute to displacement, resource competition, and vulnerability. For instance, the Lake Chad Basin region in Africa has experienced violence linked to competition for water and land resources due to climate change.

Pandemics and Health Crises

Health crises like pandemics can exacerbate existing vulnerabilities, disrupt development efforts, and create conditions conducive to extremism. For example, the COVID-19 pandemic has strained many countries' health systems, economies, and governance, potentially fueling grievances and instability.

Urbanization and Marginalization

Rapid urbanization can marginalize specific populations, increasing their susceptibility to extremist ideologies. The growth of informal settlements in cities like Nairobi, Kenya, has created conditions where extremist groups can exploit grievances related to poverty and lack of services.

Youth Engagement and Inclusion

Youth engagement and inclusion are critical to addressing extremism and development challenges. Young people can be both perpetrators and victims of extremism. For example, Nigeria's "Not Another Niger Delta" program focuses on youth empowerment and inclusion to prevent violence in the Niger Delta region.

Refugee and Migration Crisis

Large-scale displacement and migration create challenges for host countries, including security concerns and development pressures. For example, the Syrian refugee crisis has strained resources in neighbouring countries, and concerns about radicalization in refugee camps have emerged.

Violent Non-State Actors

Violent non-state actors, including militias and criminal organizations, often operate in fragile and conflict-affected areas, complicating development efforts. For example, in the Sahel region, groups like Boko Haram and various rebel factions have disrupted development projects and governance.

Pandemics and Development Aid Delivery

Pandemics like COVID-19 can disrupt the delivery of development aid and humanitarian assistance, making it challenging to address existing vulnerabilities. For example, lockdowns and restrictions during the COVID-19 pandemic hampered the distribution of food aid in some regions, exacerbating food insecurity.

Gender-Based Violence and Extremism

Gender-based violence is often linked to extremism, and addressing this intersection is crucial for security and development. The rise of Boko Haram in Nigeria has been associated with violence against women and girls and the abduction of schoolgirls.

Data Privacy and Ethics

The collection and use of data for security and development purposes raise ethical concerns, including privacy and consent. Biometric data collection in refugee camps has raised privacy concerns, as individuals may be unaware of how their data is used.

Vaccine Diplomacy

Access to vaccines has become a global diplomatic issue, and vaccine distribution can impact both public health and stability in vulnerable regions. For example, vaccine distribution efforts can be leveraged for diplomatic engagement, such as China's "vaccine diplomacy" in Africa.

Addressing these emerging trends and challenges requires flexible and innovative diplomacy, development, and security approaches. It also underscores the importance of coordination among governments, international organizations, civil society, and the private sector to develop effective strategies that address the complex interplay between violent extremism and development.

Innovations in Diplomatic Approaches and Strategies

To effectively address evolving challenges, diplomacy has to adapt to new technologies, global trends, and unconventional challenges. The key innovations in diplomatic approaches and strategies are presented below.

Digital Diplomacy

Digital diplomacy, or e-diplomacy, involves using digital tools and social media platforms for diplomatic communication and engagement. It enables diplomats to reach a wider audience, engage with the public, and respond to crises in real-time. For example, the Twitter account of the U.S. State Department's Bureau of Consular Affairs provides timely information to American citizens travelling abroad, showcasing how digital diplomacy enhances consular services.

Track II Diplomacy and Civil Society Engagement

Diplomacy increasingly involves non-state actors in unofficial dialogues and peace processes, including civil society organizations, think tanks, and academics. Track II diplomacy complements official negotiations by providing alternative perspectives and building trust. The Oslo Accords between Israel and Palestine involved prominent non-governmental actors crucial in facilitating negotiations.

Climate Diplomacy

Climate diplomacy focuses on diplomatic efforts to address climate change, foster international cooperation, and promote sustainability. Climate diplomats negotiate and advocate for reducing greenhouse gas emissions and adapting to climate impacts. For example, the Paris Agreement, adopted in 2015, is a landmark diplomatic effort involving nearly all countries to combat climate change by setting emissions reduction targets and promoting climate resilience.

Science Diplomacy

Science diplomacy leverages scientific cooperation to address global challenges, including public health, climate change, and emerging technologies. It facilitates collaboration among scientists, researchers, and governments. For example, the International Space Station (ISS) is a remarkable example of science diplomacy, where multiple countries collaborate on space research and exploration.

Preventive Diplomacy

Preventive diplomacy aims to address conflicts and crises before they escalate. It involves early warning systems, conflict analysis, and proactive diplomatic engagement to prevent violence and instability. For example, the United Nations and regional organizations employ preventive diplomacy to defuse tensions in conflict-prone regions, such as the work of U.N. special envoys in various crisis zones.

Vaccine Diplomacy

Vaccine diplomacy involves using the distribution of vaccines to advance diplomatic objectives. Countries and organizations use vaccine diplomacy to enhance their international influence and address public health needs. China's "vaccine diplomacy" involves supplying COVID-19 vaccines to countries worldwide, positioning itself as a global provider of essential vaccines.

Cultural Diplomacy

Cultural diplomacy promotes a country's culture, arts, language, and heritage to build positive relationships and understanding. It fosters cultural exchange, mutual respect, and people-to-people connections. For example, the British Council and Alliance Française are organizations dedicated to promoting the culture and language of the U.K. and France, respectively, to enhance diplomatic relations.

Economic Diplomacy

Economic diplomacy emphasizes leveraging economic resources and trade relations to achieve diplomatic objectives. It involves negotiation of trade agreements, investment promotion, and economic cooperation. For example, the E.U.'s economic diplomacy efforts include trade negotiations and economic partnerships to enhance its global influence.

Gender Diplomacy

Gender diplomacy emphasizes the role of gender equality and women's empowerment in foreign policy and diplomatic efforts. It seeks to promote gender-sensitive policies and engage women in peace and security processes. For example, the United Nations Security Council Resolution 1325 on Women, Peace, and Security encourages gender-sensitive diplomacy in conflict resolution and peacebuilding.

These innovations in diplomatic approaches and strategies reflect the changing landscape of international relations. Diplomacy is evolving to address emerging challenges, harness new technologies, and engage a broader range of actors to advance peace, security, and cooperation in the 21st century.

Using Digital Diplomacy to Address Violent Extremism and Development

Technology has both positive and negative impacts on extremism and development. Digital diplomacy offers governments, international organizations, and civil society unique tools to navigate these challenges. Here is how technology and digital diplomacy play a crucial role:

Countering Extremist Propaganda

Extremist groups use the internet and social media to spread propaganda and recruit followers. Technology enables governments and civil society to monitor and counter extremist narratives online. Diplomats and government agencies can use digital diplomacy to engage in online conversations, promote counter-narratives, and build relationships with communities vulnerable to extremism.

Early Warning and Data Analysis

Advanced data analytics and machine learning can help identify patterns and early warning signs of extremism and conflicts. Digital diplomacy can give data-driven insights that inform policy decisions, allocate resources effectively, and engage in preventive diplomacy in conflict-prone regions.

Education and Awareness

Digital platforms offer opportunities for online education and awareness campaigns that can counter extremist ideologies and promote critical thinking. At the same time, digital diplomacy helps diplomats collaborate with tech companies, educational institutions, and civil society to develop online educational content and awareness campaigns addressing the root causes of extremism.

Conflict Resolution and Peacebuilding

Technology, such as virtual reality and data visualization, can facilitate conflict resolution by providing immersive experiences and enhancing communication. Digital diplomacy supports virtual diplomatic meetings and digital platforms that unite conflicting parties for negotiations and peacebuilding, overcoming geographical barriers.

Development Initiatives

Technology, including fintech and mobile apps, can improve access to financial services, education, and healthcare in underdeveloped regions. Digital diplomacy supports efforts to promote international cooperation in providing technology-based solutions to development challenges, fostering innovation and capacity-building partnerships.

Crisis Response and Humanitarian Aid

Technology platforms can facilitate the rapid delivery of humanitarian aid and emergency response efforts in conflict zones and disaster-affected areas. Diplomatic channels can coordinate international humanitarian efforts, ensuring efficient aid delivery and cooperation among multiple actors.

Digital Governance and Transparency

Technology can enhance governance by promoting transparency, account-ability, and citizen engagement in decision-making processes. Diplomats can advocate for digital governance principles and support governments in implementing technology-driven reforms that reduce corruption and improve public services.

Cybersecurity and Digital Threats

As technology advances, so do cyber threats. Diplomacy is essential in addressing these threats and promoting international norms for responsible behaviour in cyberspace. Diplomatic efforts include negotiations and agreements to prevent cyber conflicts, protect critical infrastructure, and address cybercrime.

Cultural Exchange and People-to-People Connections

Technology enables cultural exchange and people-to-people connections, fostering understanding and reducing stereotypes and biases. Diplomats can use digital platforms to promote cultural exchanges, connect with local communities, and enhance cross-cultural communication.

Data Privacy and Ethics

As technology collects vast amounts of data, privacy and ethical consider-ations become critical in diplomacy, particularly in countering extremism. Diplomats can engage in international discussions and negotiations to establish standards for data privacy and the ethical use of technology in countering extremism and promoting development.

While technology and digital diplomacy offer numerous opportunities, they also come with privacy, misinformation, and security challenges. Effective strategies must balance these factors to harness technology's full potential in addressing violent extremism and promoting development. Diplomacy shapes international norms and cooperation in this evolving digital landscape.

Review Questions

1. How do integrated approaches in diplomacy aim to address both violent extremism and development challenges simultaneously?
   What are some key emerging trends and challenges in addressing extremism and development?

2. How do innovations in diplomatic approaches, such as digital and vaccine diplomacy, contribute to addressing global challenges?

3. What role does digital diplomacy play in countering extremist propaganda and promoting peacebuilding?

4. What ethical considerations should diplomats consider when dealing with data privacy in the digital age?

Discussion Points

1. Discuss digital diplomacy's potential benefits and drawbacks in addressing extremism and development, considering privacy, misinformation, and cybersecurity issues.
2. Explore the role of technology in preventive diplomacy, especially in early warning systems and data analysis, and its impact on conflict prevention.
3. Examine how cultural diplomacy can enhance mutual understanding and reduce stereotypes and biases in addressing extremism and development.
4. Debate the effectiveness of gender diplomacy in promoting gender equality and women's empowerment in diplomatic efforts related to security and development.
5. Discuss the challenges of ensuring ethical data use in diplomatic initiatives, particularly in preventing violent extremism and addressing development issues.

CHAPTER SEVEN: FIREARMS PROLIFERATION: IMPACT, HUMAN RIGHTS, AND COMPLEX CHALLENGES

Summary of Chapter Seven

1. Weaponization and Spread of Violent Extremism: Firearms proliferation increases homicides and violence, with "weaponization" describing situations where firearms are easily accessible, leading to harm and intimidation. International initiatives like the Firearms Protocol and Arms Trade Treaty aim to address this issue.

2. The Relationship Between Firearms and Human Rights: Firearms play a dual role in human rights; they can protect but also violate them. A report highlighted how firearms contribute to violence and psychological trauma, emphasizing the need for comprehensive regulations.

3. Differing Viewpoints of Firearms and Implications for Gun Control Policy: There are polarized views on firearms, exemplified by Amnesty International's stance on gun violence and the NRA's assertion of a constitutional right to bear arms. The debate raises questions about self-defence, human rights, and state authority.

4. Firearms, Gender, and Youth: Firearms-related violence affects genders

differently, with firearms often used to intimidate women. Additionally, homicides disproportionately impact youth, which affects society's safety.

5. Impacts on Healthcare Facilities and Workers – Primary and Secondary Trauma: Healthcare facilities and workers face challenges due to armed violence, including resource strains and primary trauma from attacks. The emotional impact on healthcare workers, known as secondary trauma, affects their well-being.

6. Domestic Crime: Firearms increase the risk of lethal confrontations in interpersonal conflicts and contribute to domestic violence. The illicit proliferation and trafficking of firearms often lead to criminals possessing more lethal weapons than law enforcement.

7. Regulation of Firearm Manufacture and Use: Weak normative frameworks and legislative gaps in firearm regulation pose challenges. Criminals may access firearms more easily in regions with lax regulations, contributing to domestic crime.

8. Organized Crime and Illicit Trafficking and Criminal Use of Firearms: Firearms are central to organized criminal activities, facilitating power acquisition and illegal trade—the consequences of illicit firearms trafficking impact development and security.

9. Terrorism: Firearms are increasingly used in terrorist attacks, contributing to higher fatalities. The availability of illicit firearms enhances the threat of terrorism globally.

10. Growth of Private Security Companies: Private security companies are on the rise, driven by fear and insecurity. The commodification of security can increase inequality, self-defence groups, and regulation challenges.

Weaponization and Spread of Violent Extremism

The impact of firearms proliferation becomes most apparent in conflicts and criminal activities, primarily through the alarming number of homicides and other violent deaths. Understanding these consequences is essential for preventing, reducing, and eliminating firearm violence. The 'weaponization' describes the broader impact of firearms on societies. It refers to situations where firearms are easily accessible within a state or community and readily available to individuals who may use them for political or criminal purposes, causing harm or intimidation.

Firearms and development have been at the forefront of campaigns to reduce armed violence. These efforts culminated in the adoption of international instruments like the Firearms Protocol, the Program of Action on Small Arms (PoA) in 2001, and the Arms Trade Treaty in 2014. These initiatives were driven by a shared concern for the immense human suffering caused by the widespread availability and misuse of firearms. They equally recognize the broader repercussions of firearms on development and society. The Small Arms Survey 2003: "Development Denied" presented a relatively comprehensive analysis of the links between armed violence and human development. Since then, research in this field has substantially advanced, particularly in alignment with the Millennium Development Goals and, more recently, the 2030 Agenda for Sustainable Development.

The Relationship Between Firearms and Human Rights

The relationship between firearms and human rights is intricate. Firearms play a crucial role in law enforcement and military operations, protecting human rights and security. Simultaneously, they are frequently employed to violate human rights. In 2015, the Human Rights Council requested the High Commissioner of Human Rights to compile a report on the effective regulation of civilian acquisition, possession, and use of firearms. The objective was to assess how such regulations protect human rights, particularly the right to life and personal security, and to identify best practices that may guide states in developing relevant national regulations. The report, published in 2016, was developed in collaboration with states, United Nations agencies, international organizations, national human rights institutions, and non-governmental organizations, using a standardized questionnaire. The report's key findings were as follows:

- Firearms are widely recognized as the primary tool used to commit acts of violence and crime.
- The Secretariat of the Geneva Declaration on Armed Violence and Development found that at least 754,000 individuals suffer non-fatal firearms injuries annually.
- Firearms have long-term non-physical consequences, such as psychological trauma and stress resulting from threats or exposure to firearm violence.
- Firearms were considered the primary medium through which human rights violations and abuses occurred, and the proliferation of firearms often fueled violence.

Illicit firearms trafficking and violence have adverse effects on security and development, directly jeopardizing the achievement of the United Nations Sustainable Development Goals, especially SDG 16, which aims to promote peaceful and inclusive societies, provide universal access to justice, and establish effective, accountable, and inclusive institutions at all levels. Accordingly, the complex relationship between firearms, human rights, and development requires a balanced understanding. Firearms serve both protective and destructive roles, and their impact extends beyond physical harm to encompass psychological and societal consequences. Addressing these multifaceted challenges necessitates comprehensive regulations, international cooperation, and a commitment to peace and security for all.

Differing Viewpoints of Firearms and Implications for Gun Control Policy

Differing viewpoints on firearms lead to polarized positions, as demonstrated by the stances of two prominent non-governmental organizations (NGOs) involved in this field. On one hand, Amnesty International, in their publication 'Gun Violence - Key facts,' argues that gun violence infringes upon various rights, including the right to life, personal security, and freedom of expression. On the other hand, lobbying groups such as the United States

National Rifle Association (NRA) assert that the possession and bearing of firearms should be regarded as a constitutional right under the Second Amendment of the US Constitution. They contend that self-defence is a fundamental human right. The NRA's controversial position sparked numerous debates, particularly concerning who indeed defends the Second Amendment and the role the NRA played in shaping firearms legislation. Although these debates are more predominant in the United States, they bring to the fore the argument of whether the constitutional right to self-defence automatically equates to a fundamental human right. This complex discussion also raises broader questions regarding the state's monopoly on the legitimate use of force and firearms to protect citizens versus the citizens' right to own and use weapons for self-defence and to take justice into their own hands. However, there is a consensus on the obligation of all states to enact national legislation and measures to regulate and control firearms, as well as the use of armed force, including firearms usage by police forces. These regulations should align with and fully respect international human rights instruments and standards.

Firearms, Gender, and Youth

The issue of firearms trafficking and misuse presents various angles, including a crucial gender dimension. One aspect relates to how firearms-related violence affects genders differently. Homicides, including those involving firearms, disproportionately impact men and women. According to the UNODC Global Homicide Study, male victims are more prevalent in homicides related to organized crime and gangs, while interpersonal homicides, particularly intimate partner or family-related homicides, are more evenly distributed across regions and remain globally stable. Firearms are used less frequently against women, accounting for less than one-third of female homicide victims on average. However, firearms are frequently brandished to intimidate, threaten, or coerce women.

Women are disproportionately affected by intimate partner and family-related homicides, making up two-thirds of victims globally in 2012, compared to one-third for men. About 47 per cent of all female homicide victims in 2012 were killed by their intimate partners or family members, compared to less than 6 per cent of male homicide victims. The presence of firearms at home may heighten the risk of domestic violence escalating into homicide or being used for suicide purposes. Homicide also significantly affects youth, with most homicides globally occurring within the 15-29 and 30-44 age groups. In South and Central America, the homicide rate for male victims aged 15-29 is more than four times the global average for that age group. The 2013 UNODC Global Homicide Study reveals that over half of all global homicide victims are under 30.

Impacts on Healthcare Facilities and Workers – Primary and Secondary Trauma

The ramifications of armed violence extend to healthcare facilities and the professionals who work there. Armed violence generates significant emergencies, necessitating the deployment of healthcare workers to areas with heightened firearm-related violence. High levels of firearm violence elevate healthcare costs, straining human and financial resources and potentially deteriorating the entire healthcare system in countries with less robust healthcare infrastructure.

Primary trauma occurs when healthcare workers themselves become victims of violent attacks. A World Health Organization (WHO) report collected data on attacks, defined as "any act of verbal or physical violence, obstruction, or threat of violence that interferes with the availability, access, and delivery of curative and preventive health services during emergencies." This report highlighted that within two years, there were 959 deaths and 1,561 injuries resulting from documented attacks on healthcare workers. While these statistics do not differentiate between types of attacks, whether committed with firearms or other means, they reveal a dimension of armed violence that is often underreported.

Moreover, healthcare workers face numerous challenges, including overwhelming demands, resource shortages, ongoing insecurity, inadequate training, lack of supplies and medications, heightened anxiety among patients and their families, limited access, bureaucratic obstacles, and stress and exhaustion. The emotional impact of traumatic events on healthcare workers, described elsewhere as 'secondary trauma,' significantly affects staff's physical and mental well-being. For healthcare professionals working in regions where firearm injuries are relatively rare, incidents such as mass shootings, such as the Paris attacks, compel them to adopt practices akin to those used in military conflicts despite lacking the necessary training, thus compelling them to adapt to new kinds of stresses were initially unanticipated.

Domestic Crime

The availability and criminal use of firearms significantly impact citizens' security. Firearms tend to increase the risks that interpersonal conflicts may escalate into lethal confrontations when at least one party can access a firearm. Domestic violence, property crimes, and minor conflicts can lead to severe harm when firearms are involved, surpassing the harm inflicted using melee weapons. Countries with high crime and violence rates often grapple with the uncontrolled proliferation and trafficking of firearms, with most firearms used in crimes originating from illicit sources. Illicit firearms have often been lost or stolen, trafficked on the black market, and sold to criminal or terrorist groups.

Regulation of Firearm Manufacture and Use

While many countries have measures to regulate firearm manufacture, secure stocks, and control legal firearm possession, weak normative frameworks and legislative gaps remain problematic in numerous parts of the world. Criminals may find it easier or more difficult to access firearms on the legal market, depending on the legal framework and enforcement capacity. Seeking firearms in countries with solid regulations and effective enforcement may force criminals to obtain them through illicit means such as thefts, illicit manufacturing/conversion, or trafficking from countries with lax firearm possession laws or ineffective control systems.

This results in the increased circulation and use of illicitly acquired firearms in domestic crime, particularly by gangs and other armed groups. In some countries, the uncontrolled proliferation and trafficking of firearms lead criminals to possess more capable and lethal weapons than the internal security forces of the

Organized Crime and Illicit Trafficking and Criminal Use of Firearms

Illicit trafficking and the criminal use of firearms are highly pertinent to organized crime. Firearms are not only tools for these groups to gain, consolidate, and extend their power but also facilitators of criminal activities. Firearms also represent a lucrative commodity for trade, often exchanged for other illicit goods like drugs, precious metals, or looted cultural heritage items. Illicit trafficking lies at the core of most organized crime endeavours, with firearms frequently playing a central role.

Organized criminal organizations require firearms to achieve their objectives, which include acquiring and maintaining power to amass wealth. This principle applies to street gangs and organized criminal groups that control urban, regional, or national territories. Pursuing power may cause confrontation with rival parties vying for similar interests. In some urban areas, notably Central America, gang members have easy access to illicit firearms from insecure stockpiles or smuggled into the region, often linked to the illicit drug trade. Members of criminal organizations are often engaged in various illicit networks, such as drug trafficking, extortion, and human trafficking, heightening their demand for weapons.

The consequences of this demand are felt globally, directly impacting development. During a 2017 conference in Africa, it was noted that Illicit arms intensify conflicts and facilitate organized crime. Even when they do not go hand-in-hand, arms trafficking abets crimes like drug trafficking, human trafficking, illegal mining, fishing, wildlife trade, and oil theft.

Terrorism

The illicit availability and accessibility of weapons, including firearms, and their criminal usage are of particular concern in terrorism. Firearms contribute to these groups' heightened threat and destructive capabilities, significantly impacting peace, security, and the safety of citizens. A study by the Flemish Peace Institute, titled "Armed to Kill," reveals that terrorists in Europe have increasingly employed firearms and small arms/light weapons (SALW) alongside explosives and other devices. These findings are not confined to a single region, demonstrating that firearms are responsible for the highest fatalities in terrorist attacks.

Numerous anecdotal cases worldwide illustrate the rising use of firearms in terrorist attacks. Many recent terrorist acts in African countries like Burkina Faso, Kenya, Mali, Niger, and Nigeria over the past few years involved firearms, particularly fully automatic rifles, combined with im-provised explosive devices (IEDs). Similar trends have been observed in countries less prone to terrorist attacks. A research letter published in JAMA Internal Medicine analyzed nearly 3,000 incidents in the United States, Canada, Australia, and New Zealand from 2002 to 2016. It revealed that although firearms were used in less than 10% of the incidents, they accounted for over half of the fatalities.

Terrorist acts in Europe further highlight the growing importance of firearms for these groups. The 2018 Project SAFTE report emphasized that in Europe, terrorists most frequently employ firearms from the illicit market. However, little information is available about how terrorists acquire these firearms, underscoring the broader data scarcity issue concerning illicit firearms trafficking in Europe.

Growth of Private Security Companies

In many regions worldwide, more resources are allocated to private security than development. This trend is driven, in part, by fear and violence resulting partly from the misuse of firearms. Human security, primarily, entails freedom from fear. In areas where government security forces lack the capacity or legitimacy to provide security, private security companies often fill the void. A report from the UK revealed that global spending on private security surpasses the Gross Domestic Product (GDP) of several European countries and is projected to exceed $200 billion by 2020.

Moreover, in more than 40 countries, including the United States, China, Canada, Australia, and the United Kingdom, private security personnel outnumber police officers responsible for protecting the general public. In the UK, 232,000 private security guards were employed in 2015, compared to 151,000 police officers. The global private security services market, covering private guarding, surveillance, and armed transport, was estimated at around $240 billion in 2020, surpassing both the total international aid budget aimed at eradicating global poverty, around $140 billion annually, and the GDP of over 100 countries, including Hungary and Morocco, which exacerbates global inequalities, as societies, communities, and individuals that can afford private security investments inadvertently shift illicit activities to less secure areas.

The Commodification of Security Service – A Threat to State Sovereignty
The reliance on private security services often arises from high crime rates, insecurity, and the presence of organized criminal groups, which contribute to increased fear among communities and erode confidence in the state's ability to provide protection. In several countries, self-defence groups have emerged in response to the perceived failure of the state to safeguard its citizens or maintain control over its territory. Private security companies may become involved in criminal activities without proper regulation and oversight. Some evolve from civic organizations into criminal groups, as exemplified by the origins of the Sicilian mafia, initially formed by citizens seeking self-protection without effective state authority.

In other cases, self-defence groups are established by the state in response to growing threats, such as Colombia's 'Convivir,' created in 1994 by a government decree to support rural landowners facing increasing guerrilla activity and drug trafficking. In a short time, many of these groups engaged in abuses against civilians and counter-insurgency activities and developed close ties to local paramilitary organizations. The Constitutional Court of Colombia eventually restricted CONVIVIR members' intelligence-gathering capabilities and their use of military-grade weapons, leading to the revocation of licenses for many groups. Some dissolved and handed over their weapons, while others joined existing paramilitary organizations like the 'United Self-Defenders of Colombia' (Autodefensas Unidas de Colombia, or AUC).

Increased fear and insecurity, exacerbated by criminal groups, can result in forced migration and internal displacement, such as in the violent northern triangle of Central America.

The growth of civilian private security services and their expanded roles in many countries necessitate proper mechanisms for regulation and oversight to ensure compliance with national and international rules. Regulations vary widely, from complete prohibition to minimal regulation. In some countries, these companies are prohibited from possessing firearms, while in others, they are permitted, with the state issuing licenses to employees to carry firearms.

No specific United Nations instruments or norms currently address civilian private security services. However, the 'Introductory Handbook on State Regulation concerning Civilian Private Security Services and their Contribution to Crime Prevention and Community Safety' (UNODC, 2014a) identifies a range of international standards relevant to the security sector. These standards can guide efforts to strengthen state regulation and control private security companies. The handbook recommends explicit regulation, particularly concerning whether private security workers should have special powers or the right to carry firearms, and identifies areas where private security entities should not operate. An effective regulatory system should include a licensing system for companies and individual license holders, including those authorized to carry firearms.

According to UNODC, civilian private security services, if properly regulated, can significantly contribute to crime reduction and community safety, mainly through partnerships and information sharing with state police. Professional codes of conduct and legislation should govern information sharing between public and private security actors.

Review Questions

1. How do international initiatives like the Firearms Protocol and Arms Trade Treaty address the issue of firearms proliferation?
2. What are the key findings regarding the relationship between firearms and human rights, as highlighted in the report mentioned in the text?
3. How do differing viewpoints on firearms, such as those of Amnesty International and the NRA, shape gun control policy debates?
4. What are the gender dimensions of firearms-related violence, and how does it impact women?
5. What challenges do healthcare facilities and workers face in regions with high firearm-related violence, and how does this affect healthcare systems?

Discussion Points

1. Discuss the ethical dilemmas surrounding the regulation of firearms, considering both the right to bear arms and the need for public safety.
2. Explore the impacts of firearm proliferation on youth, both as victims of violence and potential perpetrators.
3. Debate the role of private security companies in areas with weak state security apparatuses and the potential consequences for society.
4. Analyze the relationship between organized crime and illicit firearms trafficking and its impact on global security and development.
5. Discuss potential strategies for reducing firearms-related violence, including regulations, international cooperation, and public awareness campaigns.

CHAPTER EIGHT: THE SAHEL REGION'S COMPLEX SECURITY AND HUMANITARIAN CHALLENGES

Summary of Chapter Eight

1. Sahel Region's Complex Security and Humanitarian Challenges: The Sahel region faces severe security and humanitarian crises driven by violent extremism, weak governance, economic decline, and climate change. These challenges have escalated over the past decade, posing significant problems for regional and international stakeholders.

2. Epicentres of Violence and Humanitarian Crisis: The Liptako-Gourma and Lake Chad Basin subregions are epicentres of violence and humanitarian crises in the Sahel. Issues in Liptako-Gourma can be traced back to the collapse of Libya in 2011, leading to armed group proliferation. In the Lake Chad Basin, Boko Haram's resurgence has caused instability.

3. Concerns and Implications: The persistence of violent extremism in the Sahel region poses security and financial risks to the United States and Europe. The withdrawal of international counterterrorism support and leadership challenges in regional efforts create a dangerous vacuum. The region's instability also affects migration, international aid efforts, and global stability.

4. Recent Developments in the Sahel Region: Recent developments include France and its allies' troop withdrawal from Mali, which

emboldened extremist organizations and increased violence. There were significant political changes and unrest in Burkina Faso and Mali. A coup in Niger disrupted counterterrorism efforts, impacting international military cooperation.

The Complex Security and Humanitarian Challenges in the Sahel Region

The Sahel region, stretching from Senegal to Eritrea, is situated between the Sahara Desert to the north and the African tropics to the south. This region has been grappling with severe and multifaceted security and humanitarian crises for a long time. Since gaining independence in the 1960s, many Sahel countries have experienced violent extremism. This extremism results from a combination of factors, including weak and ineffective governance, economic decline, and the worsening impacts of climate change. Over the past decade, violence, conflict, and criminal activities have escalated significantly, transcending national borders and presenting formidable challenges to regional and international stakeholders.

Epicentres of Violence and Humanitarian Crisis in the Sahel

The epicentres of violence and humanitarian crises in the Sahel are primarily the Liptako-Gourma and Lake Chad Basin subregions:

Liptako-Gourma - located in the central Sahel and spanning Burkina Faso, Mali, and Niger borderlands- has been particularly affected. The instability in this area can be traced back to the collapse of the Libyan state in 2011, which resulted in the proliferation of weapons and armed groups in the region. The influx of extremists into northern Mali rekindled the Tuareg rebellion, leading to unrest. The Tuareg people, organized under the National Movement for the Liberation of Azawad (MNLA), initially sought an autonomous state but later aligned with various Islamist groups, including al-Qaeda in the Islamic Maghreb (AQIM), the Movement for Unity and Jihad in West Africa (MUJAO), and Ansar Dine, aiming to drive government forces out of the north. Political instability followed, including a coup in 2012, further destabilizing the region.

Lake Chad Basin experienced a resurgence of Boko Haram in northern Nigeria. Founded in 2002, Boko Haram was forced underground in 2009 after a government crackdown. However, the group resurfaced with a more expansive and aggressive strategy, culminating in the high-profile abduction of 276 girls from Chibok in 2014. In 2015, Boko Haram pledged allegiance to the Islamic State, becoming the Islamic State in the West African Province (ISWAP). ISWAP subsequently gained control of northeastern Nigeria and parts of Niger.

The expansion of violent extremism in the Sahel is attributed to persistently weak governance, marked by corruption, declining democratic institutions, legitimacy issues, and human rights abuses. Many Sahel countries face internal disparities, where state power is concentrated in urban areas while rural regions remain underdeveloped, making them susceptible to exploitation by extremist groups. Frequent changes in leadership, including numerous coups, have further exacerbated the situation.

The death of Chadian President Idriss Déby in 2021 disrupted regional counterterrorism efforts. Chad had played a critical role in security coalitions across the Sahel, such as the Multinational Joint Task Force (MNJTF) and the Group of Five for the Sahel (G5 Sahel) Force. These forces aimed to combat threats like Boko Haram and organized crime. However, the new leadership crisis has undermined regional and national security efforts.

International involvement in the region began with French forces entering Mali in 2013, leading to Operation Barkhane. Subsequently, the United Nations established the Multidimensional Integrated Stabilization Mission in Mali (MINUSMA), and the European Union formed Task Force Takuba in 2020. The United States also increased its presence in the Sahel, deploying troops and establishing a drone base in Niger.

Despite international efforts, violent extremism has continued to spread across the Sahel, leading French President Emmanuel Macron to announce the end of Operation Barkhane in 2021. Extremist groups exploited the security vacuum, launching increased attacks. A key concern is the Wagner Group, a Russian mercenary organization in Mali.

The humanitarian crisis has worsened, displacing millions of people and deepening poverty, food insecurity, unemployment, and population growth. Climate change has exacerbated resource conflicts, while extremist groups have disrupted humanitarian efforts and recruited vulnerable populations. Additionally, illicit activities and criminal organizations have thrived, further destabilizing the region.

Concerns and Implications

The persistent strength of violent extremist organizations in the Sahel poses significant security and financial risks to the United States and Europe. The impending withdrawal of international counterterrorism support and leadership challenges in regional efforts create a dangerous vacuum for extremism to flourish. The convergence of security threats, cooperation among terrorist organizations, and their links with criminal groups could intensify the danger regionally and globally.

Furthermore, the Sahel is a transit point for migrants from sub-Saharan Africa to northern coastal states and Europe. Increased violence could lead to more displacement and migration, straining resources and stability in North and West African states and Europe. The worsening humanitarian situation also strains international aid efforts, including those led by the United States, which has provided humanitarian assistance, military training, and arms sales to the region.

The Sahel region faces complex challenges, including violent extremism, weak governance, and a humanitarian crisis. Addressing these issues requires sustained international cooperation and innovative approaches to security and development.

Recent Developments in the Sahel Region

In February 2022, France and its European allies, part of Task Force Takuba, announced their intention to withdraw all troops from Mali, effectively ending their nearly decade-long intervention. This withdrawal has emboldened extremist organizations, leading to a significant increase in violence during the first half of 2022, particularly in the Liptako-Gourma area and spilling into coastal West Africa. Over two thousand civilians died during this period, marking a more than 50 per cent increase compared to 2021. March 2022 was the deadliest month recorded by the Armed Conflict Location and Event Data Project since 1997, which coincided with renewed activity by the Islamic State in the Greater Sahara (ISGS) along the Niger-Mali border and the tragic Moura massacre in central Mali.

In March 2022, Malian soldiers, accompanied by Russian mercenaries from the Wagner Group, launched a five-day attack on a town to root out Islamist militants, resulting in the deaths of over three hundred civilians. This incident, part of a broader pattern of increasing human rights violations by the Malian security forces since the introduction of the Wagner Group in December 2021, prompted calls from the United Nations for an investigation.

In May 2022, the Malian government officially terminated its Defense Co-operation Treaty with France and the Status of Force Agreement governing France and the European Union's operations. Mali's military government also withdrew from the G5 Sahel, significantly reducing the organization's counterterrorism capacity. In June 2022, Jama'at Nusrat al-Islam wal Muslimeen (JNIM) killed 132 villagers in central Mali, marking the deadliest attack on civilians since the coup. The region has witnessed a notable increase in civilian targeting across Burkina Faso, Mali, and Niger.

In June 2023, Mali's government demanded the departure of the United Nations Multidimensional Integrated Stabilization Mission in Mali (MINUSMA), the UN peacekeeping force. The UN agreed to withdraw within six months, raising concerns about a potential power vacuum and setbacks in Mali's transition to civilian rule. MINUSMA has played a crucial role in dealing with Tuareg separatists, who warn that the UN's departure will undermine the peace agreement.

In Burkina Faso, a military coup led by Lieutenant Colonel Paul-Henri Sandaogo Damiba overthrew democratically elected President Roch Marc Christian Kaboré on January 24, 2022. Regional bodies like the Economic Community of West African States (ECOWAS) and the African Union imposed sanctions on Burkina Faso in response. Following the coup, ISGS carried out a series of deadly attacks, including the massacre of one hundred civilians in the northern village of Seytenga in June 2022. In September, Damiba was ousted by Captain Ibrahim Traoré in a second military coup, leading to the dissolution of the government, suspension of the constitution, and closure of the country's borders. Speculation about Traoré's connection to the U.S. military has triggered investigations into the role of U.S. military training in the region's coup epidemic.

On October 24, 2022, the United States and the United Kingdom recalled embassy officials from Abuja, Nigeria, due to a heightened risk of a significant terrorist attack. This decision followed several incidents of gun violence across northern Nigeria, not officially attributed to extremist organizations.

In January 2023, UN experts called for an independent investigation into potential war crimes and crimes against humanity committed by government forces and the Wagner Group in Mali. These experts highlighted a "climate of terror and complete impunity" surrounding the Wagner Group's activities in the country. Although the Wagner Group faced a failed rebellion in Russia in June 2023, its future in West Africa remains uncertain. In July 2023, the United States accused Wagner Group leader Yevgeny Prigozhin of influencing Mali's decision to expel MINUSMA to advance Wagner's interests. Neighbouring Burkina Faso denied involvement with the Wagner Group, but the interim president stated that Russia is a strategic ally.

In 2023, allegations of civilian massacres involving security forces emerged in Mali and Burkina Faso. Survivors of a massacre in Burkina Faso in April accused the military of causing the deaths of 136 civilians. In May, the UN released a report accusing Malian soldiers and foreign fighters of executing more than five hundred civilians in a March 2022 operation. Armed groups have intensified attacks on poorly trained civilian volunteer forces. The withdrawal of the UN from Mali raises concerns about the potential for violence against civilians, as extremist groups might attempt to seize urban centres, as seen in Burkina Faso.

On July 26, 2023, a coup d'état occurred in Niger, marking the ninth attempted overthrow of a West African government in the last three years. This coup significantly impacts counterterrorism and stabilization efforts in the Sahel. Niger, previously a significant counterterrorism partner, is now grappling with a power vacuum. Despite pressure from ECOWAS, including sanctions and the threat of military intervention, the coup leaders have refused to cede power and have declared a new government. Nearby military regimes in Guinea, Burkina Faso, and Mali have supported the junta, with the latter two warning that military intervention in Niger would be considered a "declaration of war."

Niger had been a vital ally for Western counterterrorism efforts in recent years, especially following a series of coups in neighbouring countries. The coup has disrupted international military cooperation, including with France, which moved its troops to Niger in 2022 amid deteriorating relations with Mali. The United States maintains around one thousand troops in Niger, and U.S. Secretary of State Antony Blinken described Niger as a "model of democracy" during a March visit. Following the coup, Blinken suggested that Russia's Wagner Group likely did not instigate the coup but is taking advantage of Niger's instability.

Recent Developments in the Sahel Region

In February 2022, France and its European allies, part of Task Force Takuba, announced their intention to withdraw all troops from Mali, effectively ending their nearly decade-long intervention. This withdrawal has emboldened extremist organizations, leading to a significant increase in violence during the first half of 2022, particularly in the Liptako-Gourma area and spilling into coastal West Africa. Over two thousand civilians died during this period, marking a more than 50 per cent increase compared to 2021. March 2022 was the deadliest month recorded by the Armed Conflict Location and Event Data Project since 1997, which coincided with renewed activity by the Islamic State in the Greater Sahara (ISGS) along the Niger-Mali border and the tragic Moura massacre in central Mali.

In March 2022, Malian soldiers, accompanied by Russian mercenaries from the Wagner Group, launched a five-day attack on a town to root out Islamist militants, resulting in the deaths of over three hundred civilians. This incident, part of a broader pattern of increasing human rights violations by the Malian security forces since the introduction of the Wagner Group in December 2021, prompted calls from the United Nations for an investigation.

In May 2022, the Malian government officially terminated its Defense Cooperation Treaty with France and the Status of Force Agreement governing France and the European Union's operations. Mali's military government also withdrew from the G5 Sahel, significantly reducing the organization's counterterrorism capacity. In June 2022, Jama'at Nusrat al-Islam wal Muslimeen (JNIM) killed 132 villagers in central Mali, marking the deadliest attack on civilians since the coup. The region has witnessed a notable increase in civilian targeting across Burkina Faso, Mali, and Niger.

In June 2023, Mali's government demanded the departure of the United Nations Multidimensional Integrated Stabilization Mission in Mali (MINUSMA), the UN peacekeeping force. The UN agreed to withdraw within six months, raising concerns about a potential power vacuum and setbacks in Mali's transition to civilian rule. MINUSMA has played a crucial role in dealing with Tuareg separatists, who warn that the UN's departure will undermine the peace agreement.

In Burkina Faso, a military coup led by Lieutenant Colonel Paul-Henri Sandaogo Damiba overthrew democratically elected President Roch Marc Christian Kaboré on January 24, 2022. Regional bodies like the Economic Community of West African States (ECOWAS) and the African Union imposed sanctions on Burkina Faso in response. Following the coup, ISGS carried out a series of deadly attacks, including the massacre of one hundred civilians in the northern village of Seytenga in June 2022. In September, Damiba was ousted by Captain Ibrahim Traoré in a second military coup, leading to the dissolution of the government, suspension of the constitution, and closure of the country's borders. Speculation about Traoré's connection to the U.S. military has triggered investigations into the role of U.S. military training in the region's coup epidemic, leading to successful military coups in Niger and Gabon in 2023.

On October 24, 2022, the United States and the United Kingdom recalled embassy officials from Abuja, Nigeria, due to a heightened risk of a significant terrorist attack. This decision followed several incidents of gun violence across northern Nigeria, not officially attributed to extremist organizations.

In January 2023, UN experts called for an independent investigation into potential war crimes and crimes against humanity committed by government forces and the Wagner Group in Mali. These experts highlighted a "climate of terror and complete impunity" surrounding the Wagner Group's activities in the country. Although the Wagner Group faced a failed rebellion in Russia in June 2023, its future in West Africa remains uncertain. In July 2023, the United States accused Wagner Group leader Yevgeny Prigozhin of influencing Mali's decision to expel MINUSMA to advance Wagner's interests. Neighbouring Burkina Faso denied involvement with the Wagner Group, but the interim president stated that Russia is a strategic ally.

In 2023, allegations of civilian massacres involving security forces emerged in Mali and Burkina Faso. Survivors of a massacre in Burkina Faso in April accused the military of causing the deaths of 136 civilians. In May, the UN released a report accusing Malian soldiers and foreign fighters of executing more than five hundred civilians in a March 2022 operation. Armed groups have intensified attacks on poorly trained civilian volunteer forces. The withdrawal of the UN from Mali raises concerns about the potential for violence against civilians, as extremist groups might attempt to seize urban centres, as seen in Burkina Faso.

On July 26, 2023, a coup d'état occurred in Niger, marking the ninth attempted overthrow of a West African government in the last three years.

This coup significantly impacts counterterrorism and stabilization efforts in the Sahel. Niger, previously a significant counterterrorism partner, is now grappling with a power vacuum. Despite pressure from ECOWAS, including sanctions and the threat of military intervention, the coup leaders have refused to cede power and have declared a new government. Nearby military regimes in Guinea, Burkina Faso, and Mali have supported the junta, with the latter two warning that military intervention in Niger would be considered a "declaration of war."

Niger had been a vital ally for Western counterterrorism efforts in recent years, especially following a series of coups in neighbouring countries. The coup has disrupted international military cooperation, including with France, which moved its troops to Niger in 2022 amid deteriorating relations with Mali. The United States maintains around one thousand troops in Niger, and U.S. Secretary of State Antony Blinken described Niger as a "model of democracy" during a March visit. Following the coup, Blinken suggested that Russia's Wagner Group likely did not instigate the coup but is taking advantage of Niger's instability.

Review Questions

1. What are the primary factors contributing to the complex security and humanitarian challenges in the Sahel region?
2. What subregions within the Sahel are considered epicentres of violence and humanitarian crises, and what are their key issues?
3. What are the concerns and implications of the persistent strength of violent extremist organizations in the Sahel for the United States and Europe?
4. How have recent developments, such as troop withdrawals and political changes, impacted the security situation in the Sahel region?
5. What role has the Wagner Group played in the Sahel, and how has it influenced the security dynamics?

Discussion Points

1. Discuss the interplay between weak governance, economic decline, climate change, and violent extremism in the Sahel region. How do these factors reinforce each other?

2. Explore the challenges international counterterrorism efforts face in the Sahel, considering recent troop withdrawals and leadership changes. How can the international community address these challenges effectively?

3. Analyze the impact of the Wagner Group's presence in the Sahel and its connections to local conflicts and political changes. What are the implications of foreign mercenary groups operating in the region?

4. Discuss the potential consequences of the UN's withdrawal from Mali on peace and security in the country and the broader Sahel region.

5. Consider the role of regional organizations like ECOWAS and the African Union in addressing the Sahel's security and humanitarian challenges. How can regional cooperation be strengthened to mitigate these issues?

CHAPTER NINE: SILENCING THE GUNS IN AFRICA: PERSPECTIVES AND STRATEGIES FOR PEACE AND DEVELOPMENT

Summary of Chapter Nine

1. Cristina Duarte's Perspective

- Emphasizes the significance of the African Union Master Road Map, "Lusaka Road Map," for silencing guns in Africa by 2020.
- Highlights the interplay between peace, security, and development in addressing conflict.
- It stresses the importance of distinguishing between internal and external factors contributing to conflicts and advocates for accelerated integration and providing services across territories as essential elements in conflict prevention.

2. Mohamed Ibn Chambas' Perspective

- It focuses on achieving peace in Africa by 2020 through the "Silencing the Guns" initiative and highlights the challenges faced by Africa, including economic shocks, wealth disparities, and the impact of the COVID-19 pandemic, and advocates for a people-centred approach, investment in various sectors, and addressing illicit financial flows.

- Emphasizes the potential of digital technologies, sustainable industrialization, and the African Continental Free Trade Area.

3. Mirko Manzoni's Perspective

- He discussed the successful implementation of the Maputo Accord and its key elements.
- Highlights the importance of national ownership, trust, flexibility, and a human-centred approach to peace processes.
- Emphasizes the role of women's participation and long-term perspectives in disarmament and reintegration.
- Values the contributions of regional organizations in fostering coordinated actions.

4. Filipe Jacinto Nyusi's Perspective

- It addresses the need for African leaders to secure resources for the "Silencing the Guns" initiative while addressing the root causes of conflicts. It also highlights Mozambique's historical context, including the impact of colonialism and past conflicts.
- Emphasizes long-term vision, social justice, and inclusive peace processes and addresses challenges like violent extremism, women and youth inclusion, and social stability.

Silencing the Guns in Africa

Cristina Duarte's Perspective

Cristina Duarte, the Special Adviser on Africa to the United Nations Secretary-General, highlighted the significance of the African Union Master Road Map, often referred to as the "Lusaka Road Map," which identifies five key areas to Silence the Guns in Africa by 2020. She noted that four of these areas are aligned with the 2030 Agenda for Sustainable Development and Agenda 2063: the Africa We Want Agenda. However, she noted that the African perspective on these issues needs to receive more attention in global discussions about peace and security on the continent.

The Intersection of Peace, Security and Development

Duarte emphasized the interplay between peace, security, and development. Traditional responses to peace and security challenges in Africa often focus on addressing the symptoms of conflicts rather than their root causes. She argued that development policies are crucial in conflict prevention and resolution. She agreed with the Secretary-General's view that African conflicts are fueled by inequality, deprivation, and underfunded systems.

Internal and External Factors Contributing to Conflicts

Duarte emphasizes distinguishing between internal and external factors contributing to conflicts. While external factors, such as competition for natural resources, play a role, addressing issues like citizens' exclusion from public services is equally vital. She argued that only development can equip African countries with the capacity to tackle both internal and external causes of conflict effectively. Reflecting on Africa's historical context, Duarte noted that many internal and external factors have deep historical roots. She pointed out that colonialism's impact on the continent's governance challenges is often overlooked.

Inherited Colonial Structures as Underlying Cause of State Fragility

When African countries gained independence, they inherited governance structures more suited for running independent states. Colonial administrations prioritized resource extraction and tax collection over economic development. Consequently, African countries inherited three geographical dimensions affecting the relationship between the government, territory, and people.

Regarding transboundary movements, Duarte argued that attempts to control them by closing borders have proven ineffective. She advocated accelerating integration through initiatives like the African Continental Free Trade Area and Regional Economic Communities.

Duarte highlighted the importance of the state's provision of services across its territory. The absence of such services can lead to the emergence of non-state actors and terrorism. She emphasized the need for development policies that complement military solutions to address this challenge. She pointed to Mozambique's Maputo Accord for Peace and National Reconciliation as an example of a policy combining demilitarization and reintegration with decentralization and devolution, which helps fight exclusion and promote reconciliation.

In sum, Duarte stressed that such an approach contributes to socioeconomic resilience, which is essential for achieving peace, implementing the 2030 Agenda, and preventing African countries from deviating from their development paths.

Mohamed Ibn Chambas' Perspective

Mohamed Ibn Chambas, the African Union High Representative for the "Silencing the Guns" initiative, highlighted the initiative's goal of achieving peace in Africa by 2020. He emphasized the strategic partnership between the African Union and the United Nations, with the Council adopting resolution 2457 (2019) to support the initiative. Chambas noted that Africa faces multiple challenges, including vulnerability to global economic shocks, growing wealth disparities between nations and within societies, and the impact of the COVID-19 pandemic, which pushed millions into poverty and caused setbacks in poverty reduction. He highlighted that 15 African countries face the risk of debt distress.

The Needs for a People-Oriented Approach

To achieve recovery and transformation, Chambas advocated for a people-centered approach. Investment in education, science, technology, health, employment opportunities, gender equality, and youth empowerment is crucial. However, these transformations require substantial financial resources, including the mobilization of domestic resources and the fight against illicit financial flows, which deprive Africa of significant funds annually.

Digitalization and Africa's Industrialization

Chambas also stressed the potential of digital technologies to drive economic growth, innovation, job creation, and service access. He cited the mobile money revolution in Africa as a successful example. Additionally, he called for sustainable industrialization, the promotion of a "Made in Africa" standard, and support for the African Continental Free Trade Area to transition Africa from being a raw material exporter to a producer of manufactured goods and services. Addressing terrorism, conflict, and instability, Chambas emphasized the importance of bilateral and multilateral partnerships in achieving the "Silencing the Guns" goal by 2030. He envisioned a peaceful, secure, democratic, and prosperous Africa by 2063.

Mirko Manzoni's Perspective

Mirko Manzoni, the Secretary-General's Personal Envoy for Mozambique, discussed the successful implementation of the Maputo Accord and its four key elements. First, he emphasized the importance of national ownership, with local and national actors leading and owning their peace processes. Trust between parties, fostered by commitment and respect, played a significant role. The flexibility allowed the process to adapt to challenges posed by the COVID-19 pandemic. A human-centred approach prioritizes the involvement of people in the peace process.

The Importance of Women's Participation

Manzoni highlighted the critical role of mainstreaming women's participation in negotiations and implementation structures. He also noted that activities such as disarmament, demobilization, and reintegration should be viewed with a long-term perspective rather than as technical, time-limited processes. He stressed the value of regional organizations in fostering coordinated actions among various actors. In sum, Manzoni emphasized that the success of a peace process should be measured by how participants overcome challenges. He celebrated the progress made in Mozambique by putting national efforts at the core of the peace initiative.

Filipe Jacinto Nyusi's Perspective

Filipe Jacinto Nyusi, President of Mozambique and Council President for March, emphasized the importance of African leaders believing in the possibility of achieving peace on the continent. He highlighted the need for African leaders to secure the necessary resources to fast-track the "Silencing the Guns" initiative while addressing the underlying causes of conflicts in Africa's development process.

President Nyusi advised that Africa should refrain from yielding to agendas that seek to exploit Africa's resources, citing Mozambique's history of independence achieved through armed struggle. He mentioned the Lusaka agreements in 1974, which led to Mozambique's independence, due to negotiations when colonial rule refused dialogue. He also highlighted Mozambique's challenges, including a 16-year war of aggression by neighbouring regimes.

Nyusi drew attention to the Peace and National Reconciliation Agreement, known as the Maputo Agreement, signed in August 2019, which includes a military component involving disarmament, demobilization, and reintegration, directly related to "Silencing the Guns."

The Need for Long-Term Development Vision

He emphasized the importance of a long-term vision for the country's development and sustainably promoting social justice. He underlined the significance of the ongoing peace process, which encourages tolerance, national ownership, and dialogue, highlighting his direct conversations with opposition leader Afonso Dhlakama. He emphasized the need to address violent extremism, include women and youth in peace processes, and ensure social stability by creating opportunities for human capital development.

Carlos Marcio Cozendey's Perspective

Carlos Marcio Cozendey, Secretary of State for Multilateral Political Affairs of Brazil, discussed ongoing conflicts, constitutional ruptures, and the advancement of militant groups in parts of Africa and welcomed the African Union's commitment to the initiative and the continent's resolve to promote political and diplomatic solutions, citing examples like the Multinational Joint Task Force in the Lake Chad Basin and the Group of Five for the Sahel (G5 Sahel) Joint Task Force.

Cozendey stressed the importance of international assistance in ensuring the success of such initiatives. He highlighted that official development assistance (ODA) is a temporary solution. He advocated for a global economic, financial, and trade architecture, allowing developing countries, particularly Africa, to fulfil their potential. He emphasized the need to separate development and security topics and the importance of robust democracy grounded in the rule of law.

External Assistance to Empower Women

Cozendey noted Vice President Kamala Harris's announcement of a $1 billion investment for women's economic empowerment in Africa during her visit to Ghana. However, he opined that economic development must be complemented by democracy and the rule of law. He expressed concern over undemocratic power changes in West and Central Africa and called for inclusive resilience-building with local voices and local-led solutions.

Uzra Zeya's Perspective

Uzra Zeya, Under Secretary of State for Civilian Security, Democracy, and Human Rights of the United States, emphasized the need to depart from traditional solutions to prevent conflict in Africa. She identified corruption, mismanagement, food insecurity, and repression as factors that can lead to conflicts. She highlighted the importance of a comprehensive approach, especially in regions like the Sahel and Horn of Africa.

Zeya mentioned the US's new strategy to prevent conflict and promote stability in coastal West Africa. She acknowledged Vice President Kamala Harris's $1 billion investment in women's economic empowerment in Africa. However, she stressed that economic development alone does not guarantee peace and security, emphasizing the need for robust democracy and the rule of law. Over the past two years, she drew attention to the seven undemocratic power changes in West and Central Africa. She stressed the importance of building inclusive resilience, involving diverse perspectives in decision-making, and supporting local voices and solutions.

Shakhboot Nahyan Al Nahyan's Perspective

Shakhboot Nahyan Al Nahyan, Minister of State in the Ministry of Foreign Affairs and International Cooperation of the United Arab Emirates, highlighted the collective interest in the success of the "Silencing the Guns" initiative. He urged using Africa's conflict-resolution and peacebuilding practices, emphasizing the importance of African mediation efforts. He emphasized that "Silencing the Guns" should go beyond conflict resolution to address root causes, fight extreme ideologies, and continue to consolidate development gains. He underlined the significance of aligning with frameworks like the Sustainable Development Goals and the African Union's Agenda 2063 to inform national priorities.

Investing in Peacebuilding

He stressed the importance of staying ahead of emerging threats and investing in peace, as supporting these efforts is more cost-effective than dealing with instability and conflict. Al Nahyan called for continued support for Africa's peace and security initiatives.

Liu Yuxi's Perspective

Liu Yuxi, China's Special Representative for African Affairs, urged the Council to strengthen international coordination to better support Africa in meeting its challenges.

Supporting African Countries to Seek Local Solutions to Their Problems

He emphasized the principle of seeking African solutions for African problems and avoiding interference in internal affairs under the pretext of human rights. He highlighted the need to support post-conflict countries in choosing governance models and address security capacity issues in countries under arms embargoes, such as Sudan and South Sudan. He also stressed the importance of coordinating with the African Union's Agenda 2063 and helping Africa accelerate the implementation of the 2030 Agenda.

Liu Yuxi called on developed countries to fulfil their aid commitments to Africa and outlined various China-Africa initiatives to advance the continent's development. He emphasized China's commitment to supporting African peace and security through capacity-building, technology transfer, and debt relief.

Michel Xavier biang's Perspective

Michel Xavier Biang of Gabon recalled that the African Union launched the "Silencing the Guns" initiative when the continent faced significant crises in various regions, including the Sahel, Somalia, Sudan, and South Sudan. He noted the crucial role played by the African Union in preventing and resolving these crises, citing examples like the peace agreement in Sudan, efforts in Ethiopia, restoring state authority in Somalia, and the reconciliation process in Libya. He, however, expressed concern that conflicts and crises persist in Africa, affecting the lives of its people. He highlighted the issues of violent extremism, terrorism, and the proliferation of small arms and light weapons.

The Intersection of Poverty, Inequality and Social Exclusion

He emphasized that many conflicts stem from poverty, inequality, social exclusion, and the exploitation of natural resources. Biang underlined the interconnectedness of security and development and the need for both aspects to be considered in implementing the "Silencing the Guns" initiative.

Vassily A. Nebenzia's Perspective

Vassily A. Nebenzia of the Russian Federation noted that the causes of many current conflicts in Africa are rooted in colonialism, slavery, and the exploitation of natural resources. He highlighted the importance of avoiding the arbitrary linkage of development and security issues, as this diverts resources from development efforts. He underlined the need for the international community to assist African nations through technology transfer, expertise sharing, and infrastructure reconstruction. He emphasized the importance of fulfilling aid commitments to Africa and supporting the continent's peace and security through capacity-building and technology transfer.

Ishikane Kimihiro's Perspective

Ishikane Kimihiro of Japan highlighted the vulnerability of state and local institutions as fundamental causes of conflicts and terrorism. Preventing the creation of environments that attract extremism is crucial, and community-oriented policing models can play a significant role. Kimihiro emphasized the importance of African ownership, supported by international partnerships, in addressing root causes and fostering lasting peace. He mentioned Japan's support for African peacekeeping efforts through capacity-building and contributions to the African Union Peace Fund. Kimihiro also noted Japan's efforts in sharing good examples of community-oriented policing among security sector officials from African countries.

Francesca Maria Gatt's Perspective

Francesca Maria Gatt of Malta emphasized the interconnection between peace and sustainable development, stressing that there can be no sustainable development without peace and vice versa. She highlighted the importance of involving young women and men in decision-making and peace processes, recognizing them as actors of change. Gatt underscored the significance of gender equality and women's empowerment in achieving sustainable peace, especially in conflict and post-conflict situations. She noted the crucial roles of religious and traditional leaders in promoting women's leadership in their communities. Gatt also called for development policies to address the root causes of conflict and stressed the impacts of climate change, conflict, and food insecurity on Africa's vulnerability.

Andrés Efren Montalvo Sosa's Perspective

Andrés Efren Montalvo Sosa of Ecuador commended the "Silence the Guns" initiative and highlighted the importance of addressing the trafficking of small arms and light weapons as a fundamental step towards peace. He emphasized the role of the United Nations Office on Drugs and Crime

(UNODC), regional organizations like the Economic Community of West African States (ECOWAS), and peacekeeping operations in checking illicit arms transfers. He also emphasized the differentiated impacts of arms trafficking on women and girls and the importance of promoting the role of women and young people in peace processes.

James Kariuki's Perspective

James Kariuki of the United Kingdom highlighted the significance of development in preventing conflict, emphasizing that well-executed development is the best way to prevent conflict and its associated human and financial costs. He underscored the need for holistic solutions that combine the United Nations' and African Union's development expertise. He called for addressing the root causes of conflict based on holistic analysis and integrated solutions, involving partnerships between the United Nations, the African Union, the African Development Bank, the World Bank, and other regional partners. Kariuki also highlighted the importance of women's empowerment and youth involvement in fostering lasting peace and inclusive communities.

These statements collectively emphasize the interconnectedness of peace, security, and development in Africa and the need for comprehensive, long-term approaches to address the root causes of conflicts on the continent. They also highlight the importance of African ownership, international partnerships, and the involvement of women and youth in peace processes and development efforts.

Review Questions

1. What are the five critical areas identified in the "Lusaka Road Map" for silencing guns in Africa?
2. How does Mohamed Ibn Chambas suggest addressing economic challenges and achieving recovery in Africa?
3. What critical elements of the Maputo Accord for Peace and National

Reconciliation are discussed by Mirko Manzoni?

4. How does Filipe Jacinto Nyusi connect Mozambique's historical context to peace and development?

5. What role does regional ownership play in the success of peace processes, as highlighted by the perspectives?

Discussion Points

1. Discuss the interconnectedness of peace, security, and development in Africa, as various speakers in the text emphasize.

2. Explore the significance of national ownership and trust in peace processes, as highlighted by Mirko Manzoni. How can these elements be fostered in conflict resolution efforts?

3. Assess the role of technology, sustainable industrialization, and regional economic integration in advancing peace and development in Africa, as discussed in Mohamed Ibn Chambas' perspective.

4. Consider the importance of women's empowerment, youth inclusion, and social justice in achieving lasting peace, as emphasized by Filipe Jacinto Nyusi. How can these elements be prioritized in conflict resolution strategies?

5. Reflect on the challenges and opportunities in addressing the root causes of conflicts in Africa and the role of international partnerships and development initiatives in supporting these efforts.

CHAPTER TEN: ARMS PROLIFERATION AND THE GLOBAL IMPACT OF TRANSNATIONAL ORGANIZED CRIME

Summary of Chapter Ten

1. Gains to Violent Extremist Groups from the Fall of Libya:

- Arms Proliferation in Libya: Following the Arab Spring uprisings in Libya, unsecured arms stockpiles became a concern, leading to the proliferation of arms in the region.
- Impact on Various Regions: Illicit arms from Libya flowed into Mali, Sinai, Gaza, Niger, Nigeria, and Syria, affecting conflict dynamics differently.
- Origin of Arms: The arms market in Libya was primarily due to the stockpiles established by Colonel Gadhafi, both by the government and foreign support to opposition groups.
- Decline in Arms Trafficking: Arms trafficking from Libya began to decrease after 2013 due to national and international efforts and increased conflict within Libya.

2. Niger:

- Transit Route for Arms: Niger experienced an influx of arms trafficking from Libya, particularly in 2011 and 2012, leading to weapons proliferation within the country.
- Interceptions: Authorities in Niger intercepted convoys containing arms, including antiaircraft missiles and rockets, intended for Mali.
- Impact on Security: Arms from Libya contributed to increased armed robberies, especially in northern Niger and Mali.

3. Tunisia and Algeria:

- Arms Trafficking from Libya: Libyan arms contributed to terrorist attacks in Tunisia, with the Trafficking beginning during the 2011 war and continuing afterwards.
- Limited Demand in Tunisia: While arms trafficking increased, limited demand in Tunisia resulted in fewer instances than in neighbouring countries.
- Impact on Algeria: Algeria also faced challenges related to arms proliferation, raising concerns about weapons falling into the wrong hands.

4. Egypt:

- Smuggling to Sinai and Gaza: Smugglers utilized Egypt's poorly secured western border to traffic arms from Libya to the Sinai and Gaza.
- Economic Incentives: High prices in Gaza attracted smugglers, leading to the purchase of Libyan weapons by individuals involved in the Sinai conflict.
- Security Concerns: The proliferation of Libyan arms in the Sinai posed a security challenge, with opposition groups reportedly amassing sufficient weaponry to challenge the Egyptian army.

5. Sub-Saharan Africa:

- Arms Proliferation: There were reports of arms proliferation from Libya into several African countries, including the Central African Republic, Chad, Côte d'Ivoire, Nigeria, Somalia, and Sudan.
- Boko Haram and Banditry: Boko Haram in the Lake Chad Basin region was believed to source arms directly and indirectly from Libya.
- Potential Risk: The excess of arms accumulated during Libya's civil war could pose a risk of Trafficking if the situation stabilizes, emphasizing the need for measures to counter arms proliferation.

6. Proliferation of Man-Portable Air-Defense Systems (MANPADS):

- Concerns: There were concerns about MANPADS being smuggled out of Libya after the 2011 war, potentially threatening civilian airliners.
- Libyan Stockpiles: Libya had many MANPADS components, but only a limited number were seized in various countries between 2011 and 2014.
- Untracked MANPADS: The worst-case scenario of large-scale MAN-PADS proliferation from Libya was not realized.

7. Gains to Violent Extremist Groups from the Russian-Ukrainian War:

- Concerns About Weapons Flow: Concerns were raised about the influx of weapons into the conflict in Ukraine, with the transfer of major conventional weapon systems to non-state armed groups being a problematic issue.
- Importance of Countermeasures: Measures to counter the diversion of weapons, risk assessments, and post-shipment controls were emphasized.
- Civilian Casualties: The conflict in Ukraine resulted in many civilian casualties, mainly due to explosive weapons with vast areas of effect.
- Diverse Perspectives: Member states expressed diverse perspectives on the conflict, some supporting Ukraine's right to self-defence and others emphasizing the need for a peaceful resolution and concerns

about weapons proliferation.

8. The Hidden Costs of Transnational Organized Crime:

- Global Industry: Transnational organized crime is a massive industry generating $870 billion, posing threats to peace, human security, human rights, and development.
- Serious Criminal Activities: It encompasses various profit-driven criminal activities with international dimensions, including drug trafficking, human smuggling, money laundering, firearms trafficking, and counterfeit goods.
- Impact Beyond Crime: The impact extends to corrupting legitimate economies, affecting governance, and causing numerous health and social issues, including drug abuse and violence.
- Local Consequences: Although it is a global issue, the effects of organized crime are mostly felt at the local level, leading to destabilization, corruption, extortion, and violence.

9. Diverse Forms of Transnational Organized Crime:

- Drug Trafficking: Drug trafficking is highly profitable, with global cocaine and opiate markets valued at billions of dollars.
- Human Trafficking involves exploiting individuals for sexual or labour-based purposes, generating significant profits.
- Migrant Smuggling: Criminal networks facilitate global movement, leading to rights violations and a multi-billion-dollar trade.
- Illicit Firearms Trading: The illegal trade in firearms provides criminals with weapons and is valued at hundreds of millions of dollars.
- Natural Resource Trafficking: Smuggling raw materials contributes to deforestation and climate change.
- Illegal Wildlife Trade: Criminal gangs profit from poaching and trading animal parts.
- Counterfeit Medicines: Criminals sell fraudulent medicines, endanger-

ing lives.

- Cybercrime: Identity theft is a profitable form of cybercrime.

10. Global Threats and Local Consequences of Transnational Organized Crimes:

- Local Impact: The effects of organized crime are predominantly local, destabilizing countries and regions and increasing corruption, violence, and sophisticated local crimes.
- Victims Worldwide: Organized crime affects people in developed and developing countries, infiltrating banking systems, driving car theft, and causing fraud.
- Money Laundering: Criminals launder illicit profits through the financial system, with a low interception rate.

11. Taking Action Against Organized Crime:

- Coordination: International cooperation is crucial for identifying, investigating, and prosecuting individuals involved in organized crime.
- Education and Awareness: Public awareness and ethical consumer choices can help combat organized crime.
- Intelligence and Technology: Developing better intelligence methods and specialized law enforcement units equipped with technology is essential.
- Assistance: Developing countries need support in building their capacity to combat organized crime, with the United Nations Convention against Transnational Organized Crime providing a legal framework.

Gains to Violent Extremist Groups from the Fall of Libya

In November 2011, Mokhtar Belmokhtar, an acclaimed associate of al-Qaeda in the Islamic Maghreb (AQIM) in North Africa, informed the Mauritanian news agency ANI that they benefited from the Arab world revolutions.

According to him, AQIM's acquisition of Libyan armaments significantly boosted the extremist organization. His views echoed concerns shared by many commentators, the unsecured stockpiles of arms in Libya following the Arab Spring uprisings. The fear that these arms could fall into the hands of terrorists and insurgents was expressed by many, but the alliance that booted Gadhafi out of power did nothing to prevent what was feared from happening. In 2013, the UK's Daily Mail referred to Libya as the supermarket of the world's illegal arms trade.

Libya became the world's biggest illegal arms supermarket, a source of illicit arms trafficking to regions like Gaza, Mali, the Sinai, Niger, Nigeria, and Syria. In Mali and Sinai, weapons from Libya significantly bolstered the military capabilities of non-state opposition groups, providing them with previously scarce or unavailable weaponry. While substantial quantities of arms were transported to Gaza and Syria, likely, these arms did not offer new capabilities to groups there due to alternative sources of weaponry. However, the proliferation of arms from Libya began to decline after 2013. A combination of national and international efforts to curb Trafficking and increased conflict within Libya likely contributed to this reduction.

The Libyan illicit arms market resulted from the stockpiling of arms by the late Gadhafi. Before the 2011 war, Libya's leader, Colonel Qadhafi, established arms and ammunition depots across the country, possibly intending to employ a "people's war" strategy where these arms would be distributed to militias and the population in the event of an invasion. At the time, Libya had many firearms, mostly Kalashnikovs, with an estimated 400,000 to 1,000,000 firearms under government control. Firearms in civilian possession were rare before 2011, and opposition groups also received arms from foreign states during the conflict.

The Libyan civil war, which began in February 2011 and ended in October, saw the loss of state control over arms depots seized by opposition forces. Illicit arms trafficking out of Libya started early in the uprising, primarily through its western borders to Tunisia and Niger. Trafficking occurred in remote and poorly monitored areas, often characterized by porous borders, where official border control capacities were limited, or the border officials were party to the deals.

In summary, the proliferation of arms from Libya had varying impacts on conflicts in different regions, with Mali being a clear case where these arms significantly affected the conflict dynamics. However, international efforts and increased conflict within Libya have helped reduce arms trafficking from the country, preventing widespread destabilization beyond North Africa, Syria, and Gaza.

Niger

Niger has been significantly affected as a transit route for arms trafficking from Libya to Mali, leading to a proliferation of weapons within the country. In particular, during 2011 and 2012, Nigerian authorities seized convoys that contained both former members of the Libyan government and substantial quantities of arms. In October 2014, French troops in northern Niger intercepted a convoy bound for Mali. The seized items included antiaircraft missiles, 23mm cannons, machine guns, ammunition, and 100 anti-tank rockets. A Conflict Armament Research report highlighted six known arms convoys passing through Niger along a traditional smuggling route between Libya and Mali during 2014–15. Arms trafficking from Libya to Mali likely persisted in the following years. Niger also experienced a suicide attack in 2013, and one of the rifles was traced back to Libya. There have been reports of criminal groups obtaining weapons from Libya, contributing to increased armed robberies, especially in northern Niger and Mali.

Tunisia and Algeria

In 2015, Tunisian authorities confirmed that most military material used in terrorist attacks comes from Libya. According to researchers from the Small Arms Survey who conducted field research in Tunisia, Trafficking initially began during the 2011 war when Libyan refugees arriving in Tunisia sold personal possessions, including Kalashnikovs. Although arms trafficking into Tunisia increased after 2011, the limited demand for illicit weapons in

Tunisia likely resulted in fewer instances of Trafficking than in neighbouring countries like Algeria, Egypt, Mali, and Niger.

Egypt

Weapons have been smuggled through Egypt to the conflicts in the Sinai and Gaza, particularly after 2011. Bedouin groups had long smuggled firearms through Sinai toward Gaza and Israel. However, this activity intensified with the influx of Libyan weapons after 2011. Egypt's poorly secured western border turned into a hub for arms trafficking during this period, with an increase in high-calibre antiaircraft guns, rocket-propelled grenades, and surface-to-air missiles. Smugglers utilized unpopulated desert areas to avoid detection.

Arms from Libya played a crucial economic role in meeting the demand for illicit weapons in Gaza, where high prices attracted smugglers. These arms also found their way into the hands of individuals involved in the conflict in the Sinai. Rafah on the Egyptian-Gaza border served as a hub for purchasing Libyan weapons by people from both the Sinai and Gaza. Egyptian authorities reported the seizure of numerous arms caches, including small, light, and heavy weapons systems, ammunition for heavy weapons, and rounds of ammunition for small arms and machine guns. Egyptian intelligence noted the introduction of more advanced and previously unfamiliar weapons in Sinai, leading to concerns about the Egyptian army being "outgunned." The proliferation of arms from Libya into the Sinai resulted in Egyptian security forces being "outgunned" at times. Opposition groups in Sinai reportedly gathered sufficient weaponry to challenge the Egyptian army. Arms flows also increased the lethality of intra-tribal conflicts in the Sinai.

Sub-Saharan Africa

There have been reports of arms proliferation from Libya into the Central African Republic (CAR), Chad, Côte d'Ivoire, Nigeria, Somalia, and Sudan. However, except in Chad, there have been few documented studies of arms trafficking from Libya after 2011. However, it is widely believed that Boko Haram in the Lake Chad Basin regions and banditry in Nigeria got much of their arms flowing directly and indirectly from Libya.

Proliferation of Man-Portable Air-Defense Systems (MANPADS)

The proliferation of man-portable air defence systems (MANPADS) has been a significant worry for the United Nations, governments, and civil society. After the onset of the Libya war in 2011, there were concerns about MANPADS being smuggled out of Libya and potentially used to shoot down civilian airliners. Before 2011, Libya had imported approximately 18,000 short-range surface-to-air missiles, primarily Soviet models from the 1970s and 1980s. There were estimations of around 20,000 major components of portable antiaircraft missile systems in Libya, including missiles, launch tubes, batteries, and gripstocks used to fire the missiles.

However, a 2015 assessment by the Small Arms Survey reported that only 64 items, primarily components rather than complete systems, were seized between 2011 and 2014 in various countries. These included 24 launch tubes, 29 batteries, 4 gripstocks, and 8 missiles not seized with the launch tubes. There were also unconfirmed reports of Libyan missiles or launchers appearing in several other countries. The worst-case scenario of large numbers of MANPAD systems flooding out of Libya was not tracked.

Summary of Arms Proliferation from Libya

Arms trafficking from Libya, particularly in 2012–13, did increase the military capabilities of armed opposition groups in the Sahel region and West and Central Africa. The significance of much of the illegal arms flows into the countries in these regions is pictured by the growth of existing non-state armed groups and the rise of new ones. The arms may not have moved to the African countries directly from Libya. Other regional crises, such as Mali, have contributed to arms flows through diverse supply channels to the West and Central African countries. Moreover, the excess of arms and ammunition accumulated during the 2014-20 civil war could still pose a risk of Trafficking if Libya stabilizes. To counter this risk, strengthening Niger's responses to arms trafficking, regional cooperation, and international support for arms control measures are essential. Ending the conflict in Libya remains the most effective way to prevent further arms proliferation.

Gains to Violent Extremist Groups from the Russian-Ukrainian War

Izumi Nakamitsu, High Representative for Disarmament Affairs, expressed her worry about the influx of weapons into the ongoing conflict in Ukraine, which began with Russia's invasion on February 24, 2021.

Possible Transfer of Weapon Support to Ukraine to Armed Non-State Groups

She noted that as several countries supply weapon systems and ammunition to Ukraine's defence forces, reports of major conventional weapon systems being transferred to non-state armed groups involved in the conflict raised concerns for peace and security due to diversion, spillover, and escalation risks. She emphasized the importance of countering such diversion, including pre-transfer risk assessments, post-shipment controls, and the need to safeguard and account for transferred military equipment. Nakamitsu also emphasized the role of the United Nations Register of Conventional Arms and the Arms Trade Treaty in enhancing transparency in arms transfers.

She called on Member States to follow these widely accepted approaches and stressed that all parties to the conflict must protect civilians during military operations. Nakamitsu pointed out that the conflict in Ukraine has resulted in a significant number of civilian casualties, with the Office of the United Nations High Commissioner for Human Rights (OHCHR) recording 17,181 civilian casualties since February 24, mainly caused by explosive weapons with vast areas of effect. She highlighted efforts to protect civilians from the humanitarian consequences of using such weapons in populated areas, including a political declaration adopted by more than 80 States on November 18.

Daniel Kovalik, a civil society organization representative with experience in human rights issues, particularly in Latin America, shared insights into arms movements with various groups in Colombia. He discussed the proliferation of small arms, light weapons, and ammunition during the 2014 conflict in Ukraine, which included various types of weaponry. He emphasized the need for sustained efforts by Ukrainian authorities and the international community to prevent the Trafficking of weapons and reduce civilian casualties caused by loose ammunition.

Weak Capacity for Tracking and Inspecting

Kovalik referred to media articles highlighting challenges in tracking and inspecting the substantial supply of weaponry provided by the United States. He noted issues such as dependence on Ukraine for information, concerns about weapons flooding the international market after the conflict ends, and the necessity of developing long-term security plans. He pointed out that even when weapons reach the intended recipients, they are not necessarily used in the right places and have been employed against civilians since 2014. Kovalik cited an article quoting the President of Nigeria, indicating that weapons from Ukraine have already reached extremists. He questioned the oversight of the billions in weapons sent to Ukraine by the United States and called for a negotiated end to the war.

The Russian Federation accused the United States and its NATO allies of supporting Ukraine with unprecedented military assistance and intelligence, prolonging the conflict. They highlighted the potential diversion of weapons and their appearance on the black market, warning of risks to international peace and security. The Russian Federation called for the cessation of hostilities, the withdrawal of Western support to Ukraine, and a diplomatic resolution. Also, Norway condemned Russia's war in Ukraine and called for an end to the conflict, emphasizing the protection of civilians, including children, persons with disabilities, and seniors. Norway criticized the transfer of lethal weapons to Ukraine from Iran and called for compliance with relevant resolutions.

The United Arab Emirates called for measures to mitigate arms transfer risks, prevent weapons from falling into the hands of terrorists, and enhance arms control. The UAE emphasized the need for political dialogue and de-escalation efforts. Brazil acknowledged Ukraine's right to self-defence and expressed concerns about weapons proliferation. Brazil called for an end to the conflict and a political solution. The United States refuted claims of weapons diversion and defended its support for Ukraine. The United States called on Russia to end its aggression and highlighted Russian forces' reported human rights violations.

These statements reflect member states' diverse perspectives and concerns regarding the conflict in Ukraine and the transfer of weapons to the region. Some countries supported Ukraine's right to self-defence, while others emphasized the need for a peaceful resolution and the humanitarian consequences of the conflict. Concerns about weapons proliferation, diversion, and accountability were recurring themes in the statements.

The Hidden Costs of Transnational Organized Crime

Transnational organized crime is a massive industry with globalized supply chains. The industry was estimated to generate $870 billion in 2009, equivalent to 1.5% of global GDP. This amount surpasses official development assistance for that year, accounting for more than six times the aid budget and roughly 7% of the world's merchandise exports. Transnational organized crime encompasses a wide range of serious, profit-driven criminal activities with international dimensions involving more than one country.

These activities include drug trafficking, human smuggling and Trafficking, money laundering, firearms trafficking, counterfeit goods, illegal wildlife and cultural property trade, and even certain aspects of cybercrime. The impact of transnational organized crime extends beyond criminal activities; it threatens peace, human security, human rights, and the overall development of societies worldwide. The enormous financial resources involved can corrupt legitimate economies and directly affect governance through practices like corruption and the manipulation of elections.

Every year, countless lives are tragically lost due to organized crime. Health issues related to drug abuse, firearm-related violence, and the exploitative tactics employed by human traffickers and migrant smugglers all contribute to this human toll. Millions of individuals fall victim to organized crime activities annually.

Diverse Forms of Transnational Organized Crime

Transnational organized crime is a dynamic and evolving industry, adapting to market demands and continuously creating new forms of criminal activities. It operates as an illicit enterprise that transcends cultural, social, linguistic, and geographical boundaries, disregarding borders and rules.

Drug Trafficking: Drug trafficking remains one of the most profitable criminal enterprises, with an estimated annual value of $320 billion. In 2009, the global cocaine and opiate markets were valued at approximately $85 billion and $68 billion, respectively.

Human Trafficking: This global crime involves exploiting men, women, and children for sexual or labor-based purposes. An estimate from the International Labor Organization (ILO) in 2005 suggested that there were around 2.4 million trafficking victims at any given time, generating annual profits of about $32 billion. Recent research indicates that the problem is even more extensive.

Migrant Smuggling: Well-organized criminal networks facilitate the movement of people across the globe, offering migrants "smuggling packages." During these journeys, migrants often face rights violations, including robbery, rape, violence, and abandonment, when the risks become too high. This trade is valued at billions of dollars annually.

Illicit Firearms Trading: The illegal trade in firearms generates an annual income of approximately $170 million to $320 million, providing criminals and gangs with handguns and assault rifles. In regions like the Americas, there is a significant correlation between firearm-related homicides and overall homicide rates.

Natural Resource Trafficking: This includes smuggling raw materials like diamonds and rare metals, often originating from conflict zones. Timber trafficking in Southeast Asia alone generates annual revenues of $3.5 billion, contributing to deforestation, climate change, and rural poverty.

Illegal Wildlife Trade: Organized crime groups profit from poaching, targeting animals for their skins and body parts, which are then exported to foreign markets. This trade results in $75 million in criminal profits each year and poses a threat to several species. Trafficking also extends to live and rare plants and animals.

Counterfeit Medicines: Criminals sell fraudulent medicines, a dangerous trade that can lead to deadly consequences for consumers. They capitalize on the legitimate pharmaceutical trade, trafficking counterfeit medicines from Asia to regions like Southeast Asia and Africa, amounting to $1.6 billion.

Cybercrime: Among various cybercrimes, identity theft is among the most profitable, generating around $1 billion annually. Criminals exploit the internet to steal private data, access bank accounts, and obtain payment card details.

Global Threats and Local Consequences of Transnational Organized Crimes

While transnational organized crime poses a global threat, its effects are predominantly felt locally. It can destabilize countries and regions, undermining development efforts in those areas. Collaborations between organized crime and local criminal groups lead to increased corruption, extortion, racketeering, violence, and more sophisticated local crimes. Violent gangs can transform urban areas into dangerous zones, endangering the lives of citizens.

Transnational organized crime impacts people in both developed and developing countries. It infiltrates banking systems through money laundering, victimizes people through identity theft, and facilitates the Trafficking of women and children for various forms of exploitation. It also drives car theft, counterfeit product trade, and fraud, affecting legitimate companies and increasing public spending on security and policing. Most criminal profits are generated in cash, posing risks to criminals due to their visibility. To avoid detection, criminals often move their illicit cash abroad or into legitimate assets and businesses with high cash turnovers. As part of transnational organized crime, an estimated 70% of illicit profits are likely laundered through the financial system. However, less than 1% of these laundered proceeds are intercepted and confiscated.

Taking Action Against Organized Crime

Addressing the global phenomenon of transnational organized crime requires collaborative efforts at all levels. Governments, businesses, civil society, international organizations, and individuals worldwide must play a role in combatting this threat. Critical actions include:

Coordination: International cooperation is vital for identifying, investigating, and prosecuting individuals and groups involved in these crimes.

Education and Awareness: Public awareness about organized crime and its consequences is essential. Expressing concerns to policymakers can help prioritize this global threat. Consumers also play a crucial role by making ethical purchases and avoiding support for organized crime.

Intelligence and Technology: Developing better intelligence methods and specialized law enforcement units equipped with state-of-the-art technology is essential to counter robust criminal networks.

Assistance: Developing countries need support in building their capacity to combat organized crime. The United Nations Convention against Transnational Organized Crime, ratified by 170 parties, provides a legal framework for identifying, deterring, and dismantling criminal groups. UNODC provides training and technical assistance to help trace and prevent money laundering.

Transnational organized crime generates an estimated $870 billion annually, surpassing official development assistance and accounting for nearly 7% of global merchandise exports. While it poses a global threat, its impact is felt locally, affecting individuals, communities, and nations worldwide.

Review Questions

1. What factors contributed to arms proliferation from Libya to various regions, and how did it impact different conflicts?
2. How did the fall of Libya lead to the emergence of an illicit arms market, and what were the consequences?
3. What were the central countries and regions affected by arms trafficking from Libya, and what were the outcomes of this Trafficking?
4. What concerns were raised regarding the proliferation of MANPADS from Libya, and how were these concerns addressed?
5. What diverse forms of transnational organized crime exist, and how do they impact global and local levels?

Discussion Points

1. Discuss the challenges and risks associated with arms proliferation from conflict zones like Libya and explore strategies to mitigate these risks.
2. Analyze the role of international cooperation and regional efforts in countering arms trafficking and transnational organized crime. How can countries collaborate effectively to address these issues?
3. Consider the ethical and legal dimensions of arms transfers to conflict zones. What responsibilities do arms-exporting countries have in preventing the diversion of weapons to illicit markets?
4. Examine the impact of transnational organized crime on local communities and regions. How does it affect governance, security, and social well-being?
5. Discuss the importance of public awareness and ethical consumer choices in combatting transnational organized crime. How can individuals contribute to addressing this global threat?

CHAPTER ELEVEN: MAKING FOREIGN INTERVENTION MORE REWARDING: THE UNITED STATES GLOBAL FRAGILITY ACT STRATEGY

Summary of Chapter Eleven

1. Objectives of the Strategy: The United States Global Fragility Act strategy aims to address global fragility by promoting the development of peaceful, self-reliant nations that can become economic and security partners with the United States. This approach aligns with the 2017 National Security Strategy, emphasizing the need to strengthen fragile states and empower reform-minded governments and civil society.

2. Comprehensive Approach: The Strategy, reaffirmed through the Global Fragility Act of 2019, employs a holistic approach spanning ten years and leverages diplomacy, assistance, and engagement to help countries transition from fragility to stability and peace. It builds upon earlier initiatives related to stabilization, counterterrorism, and women's peace and security.

3. Locally Driven Solutions: Unlike previous efforts, the Strategy supports locally driven political solutions that align with U.S. national security interests. It aims to address the political factors contributing to fragility and selectively engage based on national interests, host-nation politics,

and defined metrics, avoiding fragmented efforts.

4. Burden Sharing and Accountability: The Strategy emphasizes judicious use of taxpayer dollars, data-driven analysis, diplomacy, and information-sharing. It underscores the importance of host-nation political commitment, burden-sharing, and utilizing a broader range of financing tools. Programs that do not yield sufficient results may be modified or terminated.

The United States Global Fragility Act

This Strategy aims to enhance the United States' efforts to break the cycle of fragility and promote the development of peaceful, self-reliant nations that can become economic and security partners with the United States. This approach aligns with the 2017 National Security Strategy goals, emphasizing the need to strengthen states facing fragility and empower reform-minded governments and civil society within these nations.

The commitment to this Strategy was reaffirmed when the President signed the Global Fragility Act of 2019 into law in December 2019. This act called for developing a comprehensive United States strategy that spans a 10-year horizon and employs a holistic approach, leveraging diplomacy, assistance, and engagement to help countries transition from fragility to stability and peace. This Strategy builds upon earlier initiatives, including the 2018 Stabilization Assistance Review, the 2018 Elie Wiesel Genocide and Atrocities Prevention Act, the 2018 National Strategy for Counterterrorism, and the 2019 United States Strategy on Women, Peace, and Security.

This Strategy introduces a new approach compared to previous efforts. Instead of externally driven nation-building, the United States will support locally driven political solutions that align with its national security interests. It will focus on addressing the specific political factors that contribute to fragility and engage selectively based on national interests, the progress of host-nation politics, and defined metrics. The Strategy aims to strategically integrate policy, diplomacy, and programs, avoiding fragmented and open-ended efforts.

Judicious Use of Tax Payers Money and Burden Sharing

The United States government will pursue reforms to ensure the judicious use of taxpayer dollars and achieve measurable results. The Strategy prioritizes data-driven analysis, diplomacy, and information-sharing to understand local dynamics and effectively target interventions. It emphasizes rigorous monitoring, evaluation, and periodic reviews to assess policy outcomes rather than merely program outputs. The Strategy also underscores the importance of a host-nation political will, defining burden-sharing, utilizing a broader range of financing tools, and holding all stakeholders accountable. Programs that do not yield sufficient results or partners that fail to fulfil their commitments will be modified or terminated.

Recognizing that addressing these challenges requires collaboration, the United States is committed to partnerships and burden-sharing with other nations, civil society, and the private sector. Consultations with over 200 civil society experts, non-governmental organizations, bilateral partners, and multilateral organizations have informed the development of this Strategy, and such consultations will continue as the Strategy is implemented.

Fragility Creates Opportunity for Violent Extremism

Section 1 of the Strategy outlines the strategic challenge posed by growing worldwide risks of conflict, violence, and instability. International armed conflict and state instability are identified as threats to the American people, U.S. interests, and allies and partners. Adversaries and malign actors can exploit weak governments, manipulate populations, and advance their interests or extremist ideologies in such contexts.

While the United States has helped several partner countries recover from or avoid conflict, achieving self-reliance and democracy, many other fragile countries have not made similar progress. These fragile regions often grapple with ineffective governance, weak social cohesion, and corruption, making them vulnerable to armed conflicts, violence, and other forms of instability. This fragility threatens the United States, its interests, allies, and partners.

Specifically, fragility creates opportunities for violent extremists and criminal organizations to threaten security, hampers economic prosperity and trade, destabilizes partner countries and regions, and enables authoritarianism and external exploitation. Weak states need help to ensure basic security, territorial sovereignty, and the rule of law, often relying on external actors to prop up governance systems and provide essential services. Past efforts to address fragility have yielded mixed results, with external nation-building sometimes undermining local responsibility and distorting local economies. In light of these challenges, this Strategy seeks to adopt a more comprehensive and practical approach to address fragility and promote peace and stability.

A New Framework for the U.S.'s Response to Global Fragility

This Strategy introduces a new framework for the United States' response to global fragility. It strongly emphasizes prevention, addressing the root causes of fragility, and supporting locally driven solutions. The Strategy will primarily focus on the most vulnerable countries and regions, in line with the National Security Strategy, where fragility threatens the United States, its interests, and its allies and partners. The U.S. will achieve the desired results when efforts and resources are concentrated on critical activities rather than spread too thin across numerous countries.

The core principles of the Strategy include selective engagement based on specific outcomes, host country political commitment, adherence to democratic norms and human rights, mutual accountability, and cost-sharing, which may involve establishing compact-style partnerships with key stakeholders. The United States will aim to create opportunities where possible and engage with credible local partners committed to inclusive political solutions, meaningful reforms, and lasting peace.

Recognizing the complexity of each fragile environment, the United States will adopt a flexible and adaptive approach, prioritizing the development of resilience and progressing toward peace across various interventions. Conflict patterns, large-scale violence, and instability vary in geography and time, each with unique contexts.

The United States will employ a multi-faceted, multi-sectoral approach to address this complexity to enhance partner nations' resilience. Fragile countries often face a combination of shocks and stresses, including civil unrest, humanitarian crises, natural disasters, and economic volatility. The United States will align diplomacy, assistance, investment, defence engagement, and other tools to help partners overcome crises, adapt to challenges, and recover effectively.

Furthermore, the Strategy will incorporate peacebuilding approaches to tackle the underlying drivers of conflict, violence, and instability. These drivers may include exclusionary politics, entrenched corruption, impunity, and capacity deficits. The United States will assist partners in establishing durable mechanisms to resolve conflicts, implement necessary reforms, foster social cohesion, build essential institutions, provide critical services, form inclusive political coalitions, and mobilize domestic resources for long-term peace and stability. The Strategy will prioritize women's leadership and participation across conflict prevention, stabilization, and peacebuilding efforts.

Ultimately, the success of U.S. interventions in addressing fragility hinges on the active involvement of local partners. The United States recognizes that breaking the cycle of fragility and promoting self-reliant, peaceful nations must be driven by the action and agency of host-country leaders, organizations, and communities. It cannot be imposed externally, and the role of the United States is to support those local partners committed to positive change.

Goals and Objectives of the Strategy

This Strategy sets forth the following goals and their subordinate objectives, which will guide subsequent implementation plans at the country and regional levels:

Goal 1: Prevention – Anticipate and Prevent Violent Conflict and Large-Scale Violence

Strategic investments in prevention can lead to significant cost savings and better long-term outcomes. The United States will proactively establish and support capabilities to predict and prevent instability and large-scale violence, engaging in peacebuilding efforts, which include short-term initiatives to mitigate escalating conflict risks and long-term efforts to address the root causes of violent conflict and other forms of large-scale violence. The assistance provided will be attuned to conflict dynamics and promote inclusive, participatory, and legitimate governance. Key objectives include:

- To develop or reinforce local, national, and regional early warning systems and early action plans supported by preventative diplomacy.
- To address vulnerabilities and structural risk factors contributing to violence and conflict while enhancing partner nation efforts in prevention, peacebuilding, and related counterterrorism activities.
- To encourage governance reforms, improve essential services, manage natural resources, and strengthen security and justice sector institutions to enhance legitimacy, reduce corruption, and promote the active involvement of women and youth.
- To safeguard and promote the rights of marginalized groups, including women, girls, religious and ethnic minorities, and other at-risk communities, by increasing their participation in public life and providing protection.
- We are enhancing the capacities of local civil society and private sector networks, ensuring the meaningful participation of women, youth, members of faith-based communities, and marginalized groups in conflict prevention, governmental reform, and peacebuilding efforts.
- Strengthening the abilities of public and private organizations and institutions to monitor, counter, and mitigate the impact of disinformation and propaganda from actors that threaten peace and stability.

Goal 2: Stabilization – Achieve Locally-Driven Political Solutions to Violent Conflicts and Large-Scale Violence

Stabilizing conflict-affected areas is fundamentally a political endeavour. The United States will support inclusive political processes to resolve ongoing violent conflicts, emphasizing meaningful participation by women, youth, and members of faith-based and marginalized groups, as well as respect for democracy, human rights, international law, and environmental sustainability. Diplomatic, developmental, and military-related efforts will be integrated and sequenced in a manner that considers their potential political impact. The United States will support legitimate local authorities in reducing violence, establishing stability, and managing conflict peacefully. Key objectives include:

- To assist national and local actors, including civil society and women leaders, in negotiating and implementing durable and inclusive peace agreements or ceasefires, including transitional justice and accountability provisions.
- To garner support from local, national, and regional partners to bolster peace processes and stabilize conflict-affected areas.
- To enhance civilian security in conflict- and violence-affected regions by establishing legitimate, rights-respecting justice and security institutions capable of countering various threats to stability, such as terrorist groups.
- To promote the meaningful inclusion of women and girls in negotiating and implementing negotiating and implementing peace agreements.
- To expand media, communication, and outreach efforts to build public support for peace and stabilization processes.
- To advocate for inclusive post-conflict economic recovery and reforms, including the equitable management of natural resources, to reinforce stabilization and peace efforts.
- To mitigate the destabilizing influence of non-state armed actors.

Goal 3: Partnership – Promote Burden-Sharing, Coordination, and Mutual Accountability

Effective leadership at the national and regional levels is crucial for achieving sustainable solutions to fragility and conflict. The United States will encourage and assist its partners in creating conditions conducive to long-term regional stability and private sector-led growth. By mobilizing contributions from other public and private donors, the United States aims to achieve better outcomes. Key objectives include:

- Establish compact-style partnerships with national and local partner governments that encourage mutual accountability and support agreed-upon reforms to reduce fragility.
- To secure commitments from regional, bilateral, and multilateral partners to advance governance, essential services, security, justice, humanitarian, and economic reforms and enhance resilience against shocks.
- To mobilise private sector activity in high-risk areas to improve the investment climate, enhance transparency, build capacity for effective natural resource management, and combat corruption.
- To enlist the international private sector to promote investments in fragile states that are conflict-sensitive and environmentally sustainable, fostering more beneficial public-private partnerships.
- To address cross-border security threats, disinformation and propaganda efforts by malign actors, and regional challenges by developing or enhancing regional mechanisms for economic, security, information transparency, humanitarian, and justice cooperation.

Goal 4: Management – Enable an Effective, Integrated U.S. Government Response

Achieving alignment within and across U.S. departments and agencies is a challenging but essential task for the success of this Strategy. Working closely with Congress, the executive branch aims to improve operations and achieve better results in fragile states and regions. The United States will prioritize the improvement of prioritization, integration, and efficiency in planning, diplomacy, foreign assistance, defence engagement, and other operations related to fragile states and regions, which includes interagency cooperation and collaboration with partners. Key objectives include:

- To institutionalize joint interagency research, analysis, planning, messaging, funding prioritization, and execution for prevention and stabilization efforts.
- To streamline and expedite funding processes to enable more adaptive, integrated, and agile implementation and informed risk management in fragile environments.
- Recruiting, training, and retaining diverse staff, including U.S. military veterans with relevant skills for fragile environments, and deploying diplomats and development professionals alongside U.S. military elements where security conditions permit.
- To enhance rigorous monitoring and evaluation at the field level, conducting risk assessments, and establishing feedback loops to assess progress, adapt strategic approaches, or shift diplomatic, security, and assistance efforts when appropriate.
- To strengthen coherence among humanitarian, development, and peace-building activities to meet emergency needs while breaking cycles of crisis.
- To integrate conflict-sensitivity standards into all U.S. diplomatic engagement and foreign assistance in fragile areas to reinforce political and social cohesion while upholding humanitarian principles.
- To align and continuously adapt development, security, and justice sector assistance to stabilization and peace process implementation through data-driven analysis and adaptive strategic approaches.

Connecting the Strategies and Programs of Responsible Departments and Agencies

To achieve better outcomes and align with the management goal outlined above, the United States will enhance the approach taken by its departments and agencies to address fragility. This Strategy establishes clear roles, responsibilities, mechanisms for integration and coordination among departments and agencies, and processes for prioritization.

Department and Agency Roles and Responsibilities

The executive branch has assigned specific roles and responsibilities for the advancement of this Strategy, which include:

The Department of State (State): The state will act as the lead Federal agency responsible for executing this Strategy. It will oversee and implement U.S. foreign policy under the direction of the President to advance diplomatic and political efforts with local partners, relevant bilateral parties, and multilateral bodies.

USAID: The United States Agency for International Development (USAID) will be the lead implementing agency for international development, disaster relief, and non-security prevention and stabilization assistance. USAID will enhance coherence among development, humanitarian, and other non-security assistance programs in fragile countries and regions.

The Department of Defense (DoD): The DoD will play a supporting role in managing and preventing conflict and addressing global fragility through specialized activities, including Civil Affairs, psychological operations, information operations engagements, institutional capacity-building, and security cooperation. DoD will employ the defence support to stabilization (DSS) process to identify defence stabilization objectives in collaboration with other U.S. departments and agencies, articulate them in strategic documents, organize to achieve them, and prioritize the necessary defence resources. Other Federal departments and agencies will support U.S. efforts to prevent global violence and fragility and stabilize conflict-affected areas as deemed appropriate and authorized, based on their unique mandates, capabilities, and relationships.

Department and Agencies' Decision-Making & Coordination

The Global Fragility Act (GFA) underscores the need for a joint, integrated approach involving State, USAID, DoD, and other federal departments and agencies to tackle prevention and stabilization. A senior-level GFA Steering Committee, convened by the National Security Council (NSC) or its designee, will meet quarterly to assess the progress of GFA implementation and provide oversight. This committee will include representatives from

State, USAID, DoD, Treasury, and the Office of Management and Budget (OMB), with other departments and agencies participating as relevant. United States embassies and missions will establish mechanisms for regular engagement with national government counterparts, local civil society, and other stakeholders. They will periodically review, align, and adapt plans and programs based on ongoing partner engagement and iterative conflict analysis, with updates provided to other U.S. Government stakeholders.

Country and Regional Prioritization and Planning

The United States will prioritize the implementation of this Strategy in specific countries and regions over a ten-year timeframe, initially focusing on at least five countries and regions. These selections will be made through the senior-level Steering Committee, using objective criteria consistent with the factors specified in Section 505 of the GFA. Departments and agencies will also explore regional approaches to address identified challenges and optimize resources. Wherever possible, the United States will incorporate third-party data sources and indicators to inform the selection of priority countries and regions and to monitor overall progress. These sources may include the Armed Conflict and Location Event Data Project, Fragile States Index, Freedom House's Freedom in the World Index, Legatum Institute's Prosperity Index, U.S. Holocaust Memorial Museum's Early Warning Project, Varieties of Democracy Project, UNDP's Gender Inequality Index, World Bank's Worldwide Governance Indicators, and World Justice Project Rule of Law Index.

Compact-Style Country and Regional Partnerships

A notable aspect of this Strategy is the development of new models for compact-style partnerships. Through collaborative efforts, the United States will encourage mutual accountability with national and local actors by following international best practices and clearly defining roles and responsibilities, resource contributions, and expected outcomes. These partnerships will be founded on specific metrics that adequately measure institutional progress and political commitment. Metrics will emphasize advancements in peace processes, accountable governance, access to essential services, economic reforms, justice and security sector reforms, media independence, respect for democratic norms and human rights, and defined cost-sharing.

International Cooperation and Public-Private Partnerships

The United States will actively pursue bilateral and multilateral partnerships to implement this Strategy. It will collaborate with other donors to exchange information about respective programs, minimize duplication, and optimize assistance for shared objectives, which will involve enhanced coordination within various international forums, such as the Group of Seven, Group of Twenty, World Bank, United Nations, Development Assistance Committee of the Organization for Economic Cooperation and Development, and other official bilateral and multilateral contributors, as well as private-sector partners. The United States is also exploring approaches for multilateral pooled funding mechanisms, which may include the Global Fragility Fund authorized by the GFA. These funds can effectively leverage additional financial and technical support from like-minded official and private partners, achieving economies of scale. The design of such multilateral funding mechanisms will consider the need for host-nation involvement in decision-making, especially in fragile environments. Proper structuring will incentivize effectiveness and accountability and align with diplomatic and outreach strategies.

The United States will establish new and more effective partnerships with private sector entities, including philanthropic organizations and corporate social responsibility entities. These entities will be integrated into planning efforts to understand better and incorporate private sector interests and capabilities while mobilizing associated resources. The United States will explore innovative financing arrangements, such as open innovation or challenge models, where appropriate. Public-private partnerships will adhere to conflict-sensitive standards to ensure their direct contribution to the goals and objectives of this Strategy.

Authorities, Staffing, and Resources

The U.S. Government will review its authorities, staffing, and resources to enhance its ability to respond swiftly to complex and unstable environments. The Government will incorporate this Strategy into future budget requests to Congress and seek more flexible authorities and staffing as necessary. While existing bilateral and regional funding accounts and activities provide continuity over time, foreign assistance funding directives, earmarks, and other requirements can be constraints in dynamic, complex, and fragile contexts. State and USAID's stabilization efforts are often constrained or delayed in less-permissive environments, resulting in a significant gap in the Government's ability to execute stabilization activities.

The United States will examine existing processes and adjust them to achieve the goals and objectives outlined in this Strategy. Following their roles and responsibilities, U.S. departments and agencies will review their current staffing, skills, capabilities, research, and data analytics requirements to ensure their readiness to implement this Strategy. These options may involve deploying civilians alongside DoD operational and tactical elements to achieve U.S. national security objectives. State, USAID, and DoD will seek to integrate and streamline relevant human resources, training, knowledge management, and operational support platforms wherever feasible.

Coordinating United States Government Tools & Policy Initiatives

Tools The executive branch will utilize all available tools to advance the goals and objectives of this Strategy. Specifically:

Diplomacy: Diplomatic engagement is crucial for achieving unity of purpose and collective action, essential for brokering and supporting political solutions to violent conflicts. These efforts will provide a deep understanding of the complex political dynamics in fragile states and regions.

Foreign Assistance: Foreign assistance, encompassing humanitarian, development, and security sector aid, is a vital tool for addressing fragility, responding to conflicts and crises, and promoting human rights and fundamental freedoms.

Defense Support and Security Cooperation: Basic security is crucial for broader stabilization efforts and strategic prevention. In some situations, the U.S. military is critical in maintaining public order, addressing immediate population needs, and building foreign security forces' capacity, aligning with U.S. national security objectives.

Trade, Investment, and Commercial Diplomacy: The U.S. promotes a development model based on free market principles, fair trade, private sector activity, and the rule of law.

Sanctions and Other Financial Pressure Tools: The U.S. will employ targeted sanctions and financial measures to advance stability and impose costs on actors fueling conflict and instability. Treasury will engage with foreign counterparts to strengthen anti-money laundering and counter-terrorist financing regimes and address corruption vulnerabilities.

Intelligence and Analysis: The United States Intelligence Community (I.C.) will tailor intelligence collection and analysis to inform strategies addressing fragility and political instability, focusing on priority countries or regions. The I.C. will assess conflict and mass atrocity trends and risks using quantitative and qualitative analytical methods.

Strategic Communications: The U.S. will collaborate with local media in fragile regions, utilizing media development and strategic communication tools. The objective is to enhance partner capabilities in countering disinformation, reducing incitement to violence, and combating malicious propaganda through digital and traditional media channels.

Laws and Initiatives: This Strategy aligns with and complements existing State, USAID, DoD, and Treasury department and agency strategies. It builds upon the reforms initiated by the 2019 United States Strategy on Women, Peace, and Security, the Elie Wiesel Genocide and Atrocity Prevention Act of 2018, the 2018 Stabilization Assistance Review, and the 2018 National Strategy for Counterterrorism.

Measuring Success

The U.S. will employ a systematic approach to measure progress in this Strategy, demonstrating accountability to the American taxpayer and ensuring its impact. Departments and agencies will utilize data-driven methods to rigorously assess the progress and impact of U.S. engagement and the demonstrated advancements of regional, national, and local partners toward defined benchmarks and objectives. These findings will inform decision-making and make adjustments as needed. Departments and agencies will jointly develop a Monitoring, Evaluation, and Learning (MEL) Implementation Plan for this Strategy, with U.S. embassies and missions developing MEL plans for priority countries and regions.

Monitoring and Evaluation: The U.S. will actively monitor, assess, and evaluate progress toward reducing fragility in dynamic environments. Baseline assessments will be conducted for priority countries and regions to enable subsequent measurement of changes. Monitoring will encompass quantitative and qualitative information benchmarked against contextually defined policy and programmatic progress levels. Existing indicators will be used where feasible, and new indicators will be developed as necessary.

Consultation, Learning, and Adaptation: The U.S. will implement the 10-year Strategy through iterative processes involving assessment, monitoring, evaluation, learning, and adaptation. Data analytics, information sharing, and rapid feedback loops will be institutionalized as departments and agencies implement the Foundations for Evidence-Based Policymaking Act of 2018 (The Evidence Act). State and USAID will lead in developing and managing an integrated learning agenda for addressing fragility and conflict.

The United States will maintain engagement with Congress, non-governmental organizations, the private sector, international partners, host nation, and local partners throughout the Strategy's implementation. Such partnerships are vital for effective learning and adaptation. Biannual "multi-stakeholder consultations" will be convened to provide updates on the Strategy's progress, discuss challenges, share lessons learned, and facilitate research and data-sharing on best practices.

Review Questions

1. What are the main objectives of the United States Global Fragility Act Strategy, and how do they align with the country's national security goals?
2. How does the Strategy differ from previous approaches to addressing global fragility, particularly in promoting locally driven solutions?
3. What role does data-driven analysis play in the Strategy, and how is accountability maintained for programs that do not meet their objectives?
4. How does the Strategy emphasize the importance of partnerships and burden-sharing, both domestically and internationally?
5. What tools and approaches does the strategy outline for measuring success and adapting to changing circumstances in fragile regions?

Discussion Points

1. Analyze the potential benefits and challenges of focusing on locally driven political solutions instead of externally driven nation-building efforts in addressing global fragility.
2. Discuss the role of data and evidence-based policymaking in the Strategy. How can rigorous monitoring and evaluation contribute to more effective interventions in fragile regions?
3. Explore the importance of partnerships and coordination among various U.S. government agencies, international partners, civil society, and the private sector in implementing the Strategy.
4. Consider the role of economic development and trade in promoting stability and peace in fragile regions. How can private-sector involvement contribute to these goals?
5. Assess the potential impact of the Strategy on women's participation in peacebuilding and conflict prevention efforts. What steps can be taken to ensure the meaningful inclusion of women in these processes?

143

CHAPTER TWELVE: RECENT STRATEGIC RESTRUCTURING OF WESTERN COUNTERTERRORISM ARCHITECTURE

Summaries of Chapter Twelve

1. Strategic Compass for the European Union: The E.U. has approved the Strategic Compass to enhance its security and defence policy by 2030, focusing on capacity, resilience, and investment in defence capabilities to make the E.U. a more potent security provider in the face of hostile security environments, recent events like Russian aggression, and geopolitical shifts. This transformation complements NATO's role and reinforces the rules-based global order.

2. Four Pillars of the Strategic Compass: The Strategic Compass is structured around four key pillars: Act (rapid crisis response), Invest (increased defence spending and technological innovation), Partner (co-operation with global and regional partners), and Secure (strengthening intelligence, cyber defence, space strategy, and maritime Security).

3. Imperatives for Strengthening Counterterrorism in the United States: There is a need to invest in a revitalized and expeditionary workforce, enhance diplomatic security capabilities, prioritize savvy diplomacy and holistic policymaking, embrace the fragility agenda, and adopt a

comprehensive approach to counter-messaging.

4. Understanding the Complex Nature of Extremism: Addressing extremist movements like ISIS and al-Qaeda requires distinguishing their goals, judicious use of military force, communication channels, inclusion, and reform. Addressing underlying conflicts, such as the Saudi-Iranian rivalry, is essential to counter extremism effectively.

A Strategic Compass for the European Union

The European Union formally approved the Strategic Compass at a time when war reemerged in Europe. This compass outlines an ambitious plan to bolster the E.U.'s security and defence policy by 2030 in response to an increasingly hostile security environment. To effectively address these challenges, the E.U. aims to significantly enhance its capacity, resilience, and investment in defence capabilities. Unity, solidarity, and determination are the core strengths of the E.U. The primary objective of the Strategic Compass is to transform the E.U. into a more potent and capable security provider, capable of protecting its citizens and contributing to global peace and Security. This goal is particularly crucial in light of recent events, such as the unjustified Russian aggression against Ukraine and significant geopolitical shifts. Implementing the Strategic Compass is expected to enhance the E.U.'s strategic autonomy and ability to collaborate with partners to safeguard its values and interests.

A more robust and capable E.U. in Security and defence will positively contribute to global and transatlantic Security, complementing the role of NATO as the cornerstone of collective defence for its members. It will also reinforce support for the rules-based global order centred on the United Nations in the emerging multipolar world. The Strategic Compass offers a comprehensive assessment of the E.U.'s strategic environment and the threats and challenges it confronts. The document provides actionable proposals and a precise implementation timetable to enhance the E.U.'s ability to respond effectively to crises and protect its Security and citizens. The compass is structured around four key pillars: Act, invest, partner, and secure.

Act

- To ensure rapid and robust response to crises, whether in collaboration with partners or independently, the E.U. will:
- Establish a robust Rapid Deployment Capacity, deploying up to 5,000 troops for various crises.
- Maintain readiness to deploy 200 fully equipped experts for CSDP missions within 30 days, even in complex environments.
- Conduct regular live exercises on land and at sea.
- Enhance military mobility.
- Strengthen civilian and military CSDP missions and operations by promoting quicker and more flexible decision-making processes, ensuring a more robust approach, and enhancing financial solidarity.
- Utilize the European Peace Facility to support partners effectively

Invest

Member states have committed to significantly increase their defence spending to match collective ambitions, address critical military and civilian capability gaps, and strengthen the European Defense Technological and Industrial Base. The E.U. will:

- Facilitate the exchange of national objectives for increased and improved defence spending that aligns with security needs.
- Provide incentives for member states to develop collaborative capability and invest jointly in strategic enablers and next-generation capabilities for land, sea, air, cyber, and space operations.
- Boost defence technological innovation to reduce strategic gaps and minimize technological and industrial dependencies.

Partner

To address shared threats and challenges, the E.U. will:

- Strengthen cooperation with strategic partners such as NATO, the U.N., and regional partners, including the OSCE, A.U., and ASEAN.
- Develop tailored bilateral partnerships with like-minded countries and strategic partners like the US, Canada, Norway, the U.K., Japan, and others.
- Foster tailored partnerships in regions including the Western Balkans, eastern and southern neighbourhoods, Africa, Asia, and Latin America, focusing on dialogue, cooperation, participation in CSDP missions and operations, and capacity-building.
- The E.U.'s cooperation with the U.N. in crisis management has strengthened. The European Peace Facility (EPF) expands the E.U.'s ability to provide security equipment and infrastructure to its partners, adhering to international human rights and humanitarian law.

Secure

To enhance its ability to anticipate, deter, and respond to emerging threats and safeguard E.U. security interests, the E.U. will:

- Strengthen its intelligence analysis capabilities. Develop a Hybrid Toolbox and Response Teams to address various hybrid threats.
- Enhance the Cyber Diplomatic Toolbox and establish an E.U. Cyber Defense Policy to counter cyberattacks effectively.
- Create a Foreign Information Manipulation and Interference Toolbox.
- Develop an E.U. Space Strategy for Security and Defense.
- Strengthen its role as a maritime security actor.

Since its establishment in 2017, the Permanent Structured Cooperation (PESCO) has facilitated defence cooperation and contributed to implementing the Strategic Compass. Around 4,000 EU military and civilian personnel are currently deployed in CSDP missions and operations across three continents, working towards a more stable world and a safer Europe.

The adoption of the Strategic Compass in March 2022, following the Russian aggression against Ukraine, outlines over 80 concrete actions to translate the E.U.'s security and defence ambitions into reality. One year after its adoption, the E.U. and its Member States have made significant progress in its implementation. The E.U. is committed to becoming a stronger and more capable actor in Security and defence, not only to protect its citizens but also to respond effectively to crises that affect its values and interests. With the Strategic Compass, Member States share a common strategic vision for the E.U.'s role in Security and defence, committing to concrete objectives to be achieved over the next 5-10 years.

The E.U. actively supports peace and stability in its neighbourhood and other continents. As a credible actor in international crisis management, the E.U. aims to respond rapidly, robustly, and effectively to conflicts, focusing on preventing and countering violent extremism, managing geopolitical dynamics related to terrorism, and ensuring military operations align with diplomatic approaches. These efforts aim to make counterterrorism more comprehensive, sustainable, and less violent over time.

Imperatives for Strengthening Counterterrorism Effectiveness in the United States

Invest in a Revitalized and Expeditionary Workforce

The State Department faced significant challenges during the Trump administration, including mass resignations, reduced Foreign Service applications, and politically motivated reprisals against career officials, leading to low morale. Secretary Blinken has expressed a strong commitment to empowering career professionals, with numerous career Foreign Service officers appointed or returning to government service in early Biden appointments. However, to address counterterrorism effectively, the department must go further. It must ensure access to expertise within and outside the government for counterterrorism missions and the ability to deploy these experts safely where needed.

It involves prioritizing efforts to develop a cadre of experts in policing, institutional capacity building, and the rule of law. These experts can be deployed to countries facing terrorist threats as part of broader U.S. government initiatives to address state fragility. The 2018 Stabilization Assistance Review underscores the importance of expeditionary civilian capabilities. While the U.S. government has recognized this need, it has often needed to provide the necessary authorization, funding, and structure for experts to thrive in conflict environments. Ensuring the success of these efforts entails maintaining substantial in-house expertise, cultivating a robust network of contractors and non-governmental partners, and streamlining the approval process for deploying such expertise.

Enhance Diplomatic Security Capabilities and Access to Intelligence

Diplomatic Security's access to intelligence should be strengthened, and the number of special agents should be increased to carry out their work when deployed abroad effectively. While military personnel and security measures have been relied upon for safety, particularly since the Benghazi attack in 2012, Diplomatic Security has a commendable track record in conflict zones such as Libya, Syria, Iraq, Somalia, and Afghanistan. These successes result from substantial resourcing, a model that should be replicated in other priority locations. The focus should be on enabling civilian experts to operate effectively, rather than military personnel, whenever possible.

Prioritize Savvy Diplomacy and Holistic Policymaking

Practical counterterrorism efforts often require addressing complex, multifaceted issues. Terrorist threats often emerge in politically unstable environments with governance challenges, ethnic or religious conflicts, and state fragility. Successful counterterrorism strategies necessitate savvy diplomacy to navigate both local and international dynamics. Policymaking must be integrated across the U.S. government, involving officials with expertise in development and regional matters. While sensitive issues may require limited participation, most cases demand a holistic approach, considering underlying problems and employing various tools to neutralize immediate threats, bolster partners against future threats, and address the root causes of extremism. This approach necessitates experienced diplomats skilled in working within and outside the country.

The Obama administration's approach to countering ISIS provides a prime example of effective integrated policymaking and savvy diplomacy. It involved multiple resources, diplomatic engagement, and coalition-building. Both counterterrorism considerations and broader geopolitical factors guided the policy. In contrast, the Trump administration's less coordinated approach led to increased tensions, failed alliances, and potential loss of military gains.

Embrace the Fragility Agenda and Deploy Resources Wisely

Counterterrorism assistance has been disproportionately militarized due to legislative authorities and funding that favour the Department of Defense. While the DOD has secured various authorities for training and equipping foreign militaries, the State Department has received fewer dedicated resources. Most State Department funding for counterterrorism has gone toward supporting foreign law enforcement, with limited resources allocated for institution-building, stabilization, and countering violent extremism.

The Anti-Terrorism Assistance program primarily funds specialized training for foreign law enforcement. It has regional counterterrorism programs, but these programs often allocate small amounts across multiple countries, limiting their effectiveness. The lack of dedicated funding for non-law enforcement counterterrorism programs has further hindered efforts.

There is an opportunity to address this issue by embracing the Global Fragility Act, which emphasizes stabilizing fragile states and tackling the root causes of violence, including extremism. The law authorizes significant funding for prevention and stabilization in priority countries. The Biden administration should fully implement the Act and consider increasing funding as the new approach to fragility proves effective. This revamped approach should include countries facing significant terrorist threats, as they present unique challenges that require tailored interventions.

Additionally, resources should be deployed more efficiently, especially for countering and preventing violent extremism. The U.S. government has made progress in understanding the links between state fragility and extremism. However, better indicators and metrics are needed to predict when fragility will lead to extremism and identify effective interventions. Secretary Blinken's State Department should prioritize research on metrics and data-driven programming to address these challenges comprehensively.

Adopt a Comprehensive and Funded Approach to Counter-Messaging

In the years following the 9/11 attacks, U.S. policymakers grappled with countering terrorist propaganda and radicalization efforts. However, the emergence of social media and the rise of ISIS in 2014 posed an unprecedented challenge. ISIS effectively used social media-driven propaganda as a central part of its strategy, which was not the case with al-Qaeda. The group produced high-quality videos depicting heroic scenes from the front lines and distributed them directly to disenchanted youth in the region and the West through social media. The U.S. was caught off guard, and the State Department's counter-messaging efforts often came across as clumsy, such as engaging in awkward trolling of terrorist groups from official social media accounts.

In 2015, the U.S. government assembled a small team of social media, messaging, marketing, and data science experts to develop a more effective counter-messaging approach. This effort led to the creation of the Global Engagement Center (GEC), which took a different approach by focusing on identifying, nurturing, and amplifying legitimate local voices capable of countering terrorist messaging. It is advised that the Biden administration should conduct a comprehensive review of the current state of counterterrorism messaging. This review should encompass the effectiveness of the GEC, partner organizations' counter-messaging efforts, and the status of various terrorist propaganda. The administration should ensure that the GEC is adequately funded to fulfil all its missions, enable unconventional hiring to bring in outside experts and grant its leadership the necessary flexibility to carry out its mission effectively.

Understanding the Complex Nature of Extremism and the Role of Geopolitics

Extremist movements like the Islamic State (I.S.), al-Qaeda, Boko Haram, and others are central to some of the deadliest crises today, complicating efforts to resolve them. These groups have capitalized on wars, state collapse, and geopolitical upheaval in the Middle East, extending their influence into Africa and other less-developed regions. Hence, it is crucial to avoid the mistakes that facilitated their rise.

One key aspect of addressing these extremist groups is distinguishing between those with different goals and employing military force judiciously. Removing militants should only occur when there is a viable plan for what comes next, so the mistake of Iraq and Libya is not repeated. Additionally, it is essential to establish communication channels, even with hardline elements, and prioritize dialogue, inclusion, and reform to de-escalate crises and prevent new ones from erupting. Also, taking steps to address agelong conflicts like the Saudi-Iranian rivalry has become necessary. In Libya, Syria, and Yemen, efforts should focus on creating alternative orders that can attract support away from extremist groups.

It is essential to acknowledge that resolving these issues is challenging. However, it is wiser to address underlying fault lines rather than merely attempting to gloss over them under the banner of countering "violent extremism.

Review Questions

1. Why did the E.U. develop the Strategic Compass, and what are its main objectives?
2. What are the four critical pillars of the Strategic Compass, and how do they contribute to the E.U.'s security and defence goals?

3. What challenges did the U.S. State Department face during the Trump administration regarding counterterrorism efforts?

4. How can the U.S. enhance diplomatic security capabilities, and why is it essential for counterterrorism?

5. What is the significance of adopting a comprehensive approach to counter-messaging in countering extremist propaganda?

Discussion Points

1. Discuss the implications of the E.U.'s Strategic Compass for transatlantic Security and global peace. How does it complement NATO's role?

2. Explore the challenges and opportunities of strengthening counterterrorism effectiveness in the United States. How can the U.S. balance military and civilian efforts in counterterrorism?

3. How can the U.S. government better allocate resources and prioritize efforts to address the root causes of extremism and state fragility, as the text recommends?

4. Share examples of effective counter-messaging strategies in countering extremist propaganda. What lessons can be learned from these approaches?

5. Discuss the complexities of addressing extremist movements in conflict-ridden regions, including the importance of distinguishing between different groups and the role of diplomatic efforts.

CHAPTER THIRTEEN: JIHADISM: LEARNING FROM THE PAST AND ADAPTING FOR THE FUTURE

Summary of Chapter Thirteen

1. Learning from Post-9/11 Mistakes: The aftermath of the September 11, 2001, terrorist attack and the global growth of violent extremism highlight the importance of learning from past mistakes to prevent future occurrences. However, it is essential to recognize that each extremist movement is unique and rooted in local contexts, necessitating tailored responses.

2. Disaggregation Over Conflation: Counterterrorism efforts should avoid generalizing fundamentalist groups and treat each case individually. Distinguishing between violent and non-violent Islamist groups and recognizing diverse motives within extremist movements is critical to effective counterterrorism.

3. Containment When Necessary: Prioritizing comprehensive plans for post-militant situations is essential. Rushing into military operations without a broader political settlement can exacerbate chaos, making containment a safer option.

4. Respect for Rules and Restraint: Military actions against extremists should adhere to international humanitarian law to prevent radicalizing communities. Targeted killings, like drone strikes, should be used

judiciously due to potential unintended consequences and the risk of breeding resentment.

5. Dialogue and Conflict Prevention: Engaging in dialogue, even with radicals, is essential for de-escalation. Conflict prevention, inclusive politics, and addressing grievances can be more effective in countering violent extremism than solely focusing on counterterrorism efforts.

Learning from Post-9/11 Mistakes and Tailoring Responses

The September 11, 2001 attack and the aftermath remain a watershed in pre-meditated terrorist attacks and the growth of violent extremism globally. Learning from the mistakes made then will help prevent Understanding with lessons to prevent any future re-occurrence. However, a note of caution: despite the links and transnational connections of specific extremist movements, each is unique and rooted in local contexts, necessitating a tailored response. So, although terrorist groups may present similar dilemmas and propensities, it is essential to tailor counterterrorism efforts to match each case. Notwithstanding, there are everyday actions that can help contain different violent extremist groups:

Disaggregate Instead of Conflate

Avoid generalizing fundamentalist groups. Not all Islamist groups are violent. For instance, Boko Haram was initially a non-violent Islamist group before being brutally attacked and radicalized. Another example is the Muslim Brotherhood, which is willing to embrace political and religious pluralism and participate in politics. It is counterproductive to treat them as violent extremists. It is also necessary to distinguish between movements seeking a place within the international order and those aiming to disrupt it. Even within groups like ISIS, its local branches, and al-Qaeda affiliates, rank-and-file members have diverse motives that can change with evolving conditions. Governments should avoid grouping diverse movements together and instead focus on ending violence without conflating them into a unified enemy.

Contain When No Better Option Exists

Prioritize having a viable plan for what comes after ousting militants. In situations like the current strategy in Iraq, where towns are razed to defeat ISIS, and in Libya, where there is a heavy bombardment or Western troop deployment, without a broader political settlement, containment may be the safer option. Rushing military operations without a comprehensive plan can exacerbate chaos.

Use Force Wisely

Force may be necessary sometimes, but restraint should be exercised in war because there will always be unintended consequences. Pulling back after a military onslaught is often costly. It will leave scars that create avoidable pain and hatred. Lessons from Somalia and Afghanistan illustrate the shortcomings of defining all adversaries as terrorists or violent extremists and combining state-building efforts with military actions without a broader political strategy.

Respect Rules

Military actions against extremists should be carried out while adhering to international humanitarian law to avoid radicalizing communities or leaving them trapped between extremist rule and indiscriminate military operations. Jihadists often gain support by offering protection against various threats in conflict zones.

Curb Targeted Killings

While drone strikes may disrupt extremist operations, they can also breed resentment against local governments and the West. Eliminating extremist leaders may not end the wars or weaken most movements significantly. Predicting the consequences of targeted killings, especially in urban warfare or infighting between jihadist factions, is challenging.

Maintain Lines of Communication Even During the War

Despite the difficulties, governments should be willing to engage in dialogue, even with radicals. Military action must not be seen as the solution or an end. Opportunities to de-escalate violence should be looked out for and not missed. Policymakers should be present on the official front and the unofficial, discreet communication channels through community leaders or insider mediators, particularly regarding humanitarian issues of shared concern.

Narrow the "Countering Violent Extremism" (CVE) Agenda

While CVE efforts addressing root causes, including essential state obligations like education, employment, and services to marginalized communities, are valuable, caution should be exercised in expanding the CVE agenda. Overemphasizing "violent extremism" as the main threat to stability may overlook other sources of fragility, delegitimize political grievances, and stigmatize communities as potential extremists. Policymakers and donors should thoroughly define what falls under CVE and research radicalization pathways.

Invest in Conflict Prevention

Prevention is cheaper and easier than fighting down extremists. Encouraging inclusive politics, addressing community grievances, and responding measuredly to terrorist attacks can help prevent crises. Preventing crises will likely have a more significant impact on containing violent extremists than simply countering violent extremism.

Evolving Jihadist Landscape: The recent expansion of ISIS and al-Qaeda represents the fourth Wave of jihadist violence, which has primarily affected the Muslim world since the fall of the Soviet-backed government in Afghanistan in 1989. Each Wave had distinct characteristics and impacts, with the current Wave being perilous. It is driven by factors such as ISIS's territorial control, ideological innovation, and its ability to tap into local Sunni and broader anti-establishment discontent.

The growing threat posed by extremist groups, mainly ISIS and al-Qaeda, demands a balanced and strategic response. World leaders must learn from past mistakes and avoid hasty military actions that can exacerbate conflicts. Understanding the diverse nature of these extremist movements, respecting international rules, and investing in conflict prevention are essential components of a practical approach to addressing the current jihadist landscape.

Understanding the Four Waves of Jihadist Violence

The concept of "four waves of jihadism" is a framework used to understand the evolution of jihadist movements and terrorism over time. These waves represent distinct periods in the history of jihadist activity and are characterized by different ideologies, strategies, and critical actors.

First Wave (Late 19th to Mid-20th Century): This early Wave of jihadism focused on anti-colonial and anti-imperialist movements in the context of European colonial rule in Muslim-majority regions. Notable figures such as Abdul Hamid II in the Ottoman Empire and the Mahdist movement in Sudan were associated with this Wave. The objective was often to resist foreign occupation and regain sovereignty.

Second Wave (1980s to Early 2000s): The second Wave was marked by the emergence of transnational jihadist organizations with a global agenda. It gained momentum during the Soviet-Afghan War when foreign fighters, including Osama bin Laden, joined the Afghan resistance against the Soviet Union. Al-Qaeda was a crucial player in this Wave and was responsible for major terrorist attacks, such as the 1998 U.S. embassy bombings in East Africa and the 9/11 attacks. A focus on international jihad and attacks on Western targets characterized this Wave.

Third Wave (The mid-2000s to Early 2010s): The third Wave saw the proliferation of regional and localized jihadist movements, often linked to civil conflicts and insurgencies. It included groups like Boko Haram in Nigeria, Al-Shabaab in Somalia, and Al-Qaeda in the Islamic Maghreb (AQIM). These groups aimed to establish Islamic states in specific regions rather than focusing on global jihad. Their tactics included suicide bombings, guerrilla warfare, and the imposition of strict interpretations of Islamic law in areas they controlled.

Fourth Wave (Mid-2010s to Present): The fourth Wave is characterized by expanding extremist ideologies and using social media for recruitment and radicalization. The rise of ISIS (Islamic State of Iraq and Syria) marked a significant development within this Wave. ISIS aimed to establish a global caliphate and attracted foreign fighters from various countries. Unlike Al-Qaeda, which focused on attacking the West, ISIS sought to conquer and govern the territory. The fourth Wave also saw a rise in lone-wolf attacks and small-scale, self-radicalized terrorism.

Understanding that these waves simplify a complex and evolving phenomenon is essential. Jihadism is not a monolithic movement, and groups within these waves often have distinct goals, ideologies, and methods. Additionally, the nature of jihadism continues to change as new geopolitical developments, technological advancements, and ideological shifts occur. Scholars and analysts use this framework to provide historical context and identify fundamental shifts in the jihadist landscape.

The 2003 U.S. invasion of Iraq marked the onset of a third wave of jihadist violence. This invasion re-energized the jihadist movement as thousands of Muslims, particularly from the Gulf and North Africa, joined the fight against American forces in the heart of the Arab world. However, the Awakening partially halted this Wave, a tribal uprising in Iraq backed by the U.S., motivated by al-Qaeda's brutality. The Arab Spring protests in 2011 initially seemed to end this Wave.

However, the collapse or suppression of many of these revolutions has led to the emergence of a fourth and more potent wave of jihadist violence. This Wave has witnessed ISIS and al-Qaeda-affiliated groups capturing territory, establishing new footholds in Africa, and posing a significant threat across much of the Muslim world and the West. It is important to note that generalizing the underlying causes of this fourth Wave is challenging, given variations across regions and unique local conditions. The expansion of jihadists results from various factors occurring differently in different places, some directly connected, some indirectly, and others not at all.

Immediate Causes of the Fourth Wave

The recent upheaval across much of the Arab world plays a central role in this fourth Wave of jihadist expansion. Historically, jihadist gains have been closely tied to conflict, from Afghanistan to Algeria, Iraq to Syria. The recent surge in warfare and state disintegration has created significant opportunities for these extremist groups. Additionally, heightened enmity between Middle Eastern states, surpassing levels seen in previous waves, means that regional powers are more preoccupied with their rivalries than with the threat posed by extremist groups. Sometimes, these regional powers even quietly support extremist groups as proxies.

Deepening sectarianism, Sunni feelings of victimization, and concerns over Iran's ascendancy in the region have played into the hands of jihadists. Failed governance, authoritarian crackdowns, and the absence of legitimate and politically viable alternatives have reinforced jihadist narratives against corrupt local regimes and fueled anti-establishment sentiments. Weak states with limited control over their territories have proven particularly vulnerable, especially in Africa. Decades of the spread of intolerant strains of Islam and the diminishing appeal of resistance ideologies have also contributed to the fertile ground for extremism.

The grievances that initially sparked protests in the Arab Spring were similar to those motivating other revolts across the Arab world. Initially, most protesters did not demand President Bashar al-Assad's removal but sought political reforms, more open politics, and better economic management. Over time, peaceful protests evolved into a jihadist-dominated insurgency for different reasons. The Assad regime's response, marked by brutal violence, divisive sectarian rhetoric, collective punishment, and the release of jailed radicals, fueled radicalization. This pattern of jihadists exploiting chances created by conflict and state collapse, and their rise facilitated by the mistakes of others, is recurrent.

Geopolitical Rivalries and Proxy Support

Escalating geopolitical rivalries have also played into the hands of extremists. The modern jihadist movement traces its roots partly to state competition during the Cold War, particularly in Afghanistan. This competition involved the USSR's invasion, the U.S. and Gulf monarchies supporting, and Pakistan radicalizing Muslims to combat Soviet forces. Furthermore, the Gulf's increased funding for radical Sunni movements, partly as a response to Iran's sponsorship of Shia activism following its 1979 revolution, contributed to the emergence of the modern jihadist movement.

Today, these regional rivalries hinder efforts to end the crises that jihadists exploit. Regional powers, especially Middle Eastern states, are more concerned about their geopolitical competitors than the extremist threat. For example, Saudi Arabia and the UAE have prioritized their fight against the Huthis in Yemen over combatting al-Qaeda. These rivalries have led to a lack of coherent action against extremist groups.

Moreover, whether direct or indirect, state support for jihadist groups appears to be growing, driven, in part, by the escalating competition between Iran and Gulf monarchies after the nuclear deal. Some of the weapons and support provided by Gulf states and Turkey to various Syrian rebel groups may end up in the hands of extremist proxies. Pakistan's history shows the dangers of using jihadists as proxies. These extremist groups can turn against their state sponsors when their objectives diverge, making them unpredictable and potentially destabilizing.

While genuine concerns may drive regional rivalries and state support for jihadists, subordinating the fight against extremist groups to these geopolitical interests could be a strategic mistake.

Factors Contributing to the Fourth Wave of Jihadism in the Middle East

The fourth Wave of jihadism, characterized by the rise of groups like the Islamic State (I.S.), has been shaped by a complex interplay of factors. While the proximate causes include wars, state collapse, and geopolitical tensions across the Arab world, several underlying trends have significantly contributed to the emergence and expansion of jihadist movements in the region.

Sectarianism

Sectarianism in the Middle East has reached unprecedented levels, exacerbated by events such as Saddam Hussein's overthrow, the wars in Syria and Iraq, and the rivalry between Saudi Arabia and Iran. This sectarian divide has driven many, not only Sunnis but others, to seek protection and representation through alternative social organizations such as tribes, clans, religions, and sects. The consequences of this sectarian hatred are still uncertain, but it undeniably plays into the hands of groups like I.S., which thrive on and fuel such divisions. Additionally, it has led to a new generation of jihadists who gained experience by fighting Iran-backed forces in Syria and Iraq.

Sense of Victimization

Sunni Arabs harbour a profound sense of victimization, amplified by the West's focus on I.S. atrocities while overlooking, or seemingly facilitating, the violence against Sunnis by Iran-sponsored regimes and militias, notably in Iraq. The 2011 Arab uprisings destabilized traditional power centres like Egypt, leaving a vacuum that Saudi Arabia attempted to fill, partly by inflaming sectarian sentiments. However, this approach is difficult, as it competes with I.S. on the dangerous terrain of sectarianism.

Persistent Authoritarianism

The roots of the fourth Wave of jihadism partly lie in long-standing authoritarianism. Many leaders and regimes, backed by major powers, clung to power through repression and violence. While these regimes provided relative stability, their misrule eroded state-society relations and institutions, paving the way for the chaos that followed their overthrow. Leaders like Maliki in Iraq and Assad in Syria contributed to the wars that ultimately benefited I.S. The lack of prospects for reform in many Arab countries fuels anti-establishment sentiment, particularly among the youth, and lends credibility to jihadist criticism of corrupt local regimes.

Weak States and Security Forces

African leaders, although often more united against jihadists than their Middle Eastern counterparts, struggle with weak states, limited influence in marginalized regions, and ineffective security forces. Conditions conducive to jihadist movements, like Boko Haram in Nigeria and militants in Mali, include underdevelopment, distrust of the state in peripheral areas, declining authority of traditional elites, the widespread availability of weapons, and clumsy security responses.

Ideological Space

The opening of ideological space in the Arab world and parts of Africa has contributed to the rise of jihadist movements. Once-used ideologies for political activity and resistance against repression, such as socialism and Arab nationalism, have lost appeal. Neo-liberal reforms and global governance have often worsened living conditions, and the collapse of the 2011 revolutions damaged the prospects of liberal democracy and peaceful political Islam. The Muslim Brotherhood's experience in Egypt, from President Morsi's inept performance to President al-Sisi's repression, has bolstered jihadist narratives.

Spread of Intolerant Strands of Islam

The spread of intolerant strains of Islam, often associated with Wahhabism or Salafism, has played a role in fostering jihadist ideologies. Saudi-sponsored proselytizing efforts across the Muslim world have created a pool of potential recruits who share a general theological disposition with jihadists. However, it is crucial to note that not all Salafis endorse violence, and many may serve as potential allies against jihadist violence.

While jihadist ideologies may not gain mass appeal in the Muslim world, they continue to pose a significant threat. Factors such as sectarianism, authoritarianism, state fragility, and the spread of intolerant ideologies have created fertile ground for the growth of jihadist movements. Countering their ideology is only one part of the solution; addressing the root causes, reinvigorating efforts to end wars, reducing state rivalries, and preventing crises are equally urgent priorities in combating jihadist extremism in the Middle East and other regions.

Review Questions

1. Why is it essential to tailor counterterrorism efforts to the unique characteristics of each extremist group, and what are the risks of conflating them?
2. What are the critical considerations for post-militant containment in counterterrorism strategies?
3. How can military actions against extremists adhere to international humanitarian law, and why is this important for preventing radicalization?
4. What factors contribute to the emergence and expansion of jihadist movements in the Middle East, as discussed in the text?
5. How can dialogue with radical elements contribute to de-escalation and conflict prevention in counterterrorism efforts?

Discussion Points

1. Explore the challenges and complexities of distinguishing between violent and non-violent Islamist groups in counterterrorism efforts. How can governments and international organizations effectively engage with non-violent groups while countering extremism?

2. Discuss the ethical and strategic implications of targeted killings in counterterrorism operations, such as drone strikes. How can the potential negative consequences be mitigated?

3. Consider the role of regional rivalries and state support in fueling jihadist movements. How can international cooperation address these geopolitical factors in counterterrorism efforts?

4. Analyze the impact of sectarianism, authoritarianism, and weak states in contributing to the rise of jihadist extremism. How can these underlying issues be addressed to prevent the growth of extremist movements?

5. Examine the effectiveness of dialogue and conflict prevention in countering violent extremism. How can policymakers balance security concerns with efforts to address the root causes of extremism?

CHAPTER FOURTEEN: SHIFTING JIHADISM LANDSCAPE - A COMPARATIVE ANALYSIS OF IS AND AL-QAEDA STRATEGIES

Summary of Chapter Fourteen

1. Comparative Analysis of IS and Al-Qaeda Strategies: differences in recruitment, expansionist approaches, and governance styles.

2. IS in Libya: IS aimed to expand its influence in Libya, recruiting from local groups and exploiting security vacuums. It managed to gain control over a significant coastal stretch around Sirte by forming alliances with local leaders.

3. IS in Various Regions: The text explores IS's presence and activities in Egypt's Sinai region, Yemen, Afghanistan, Russia's North Caucasus, and the Chad Basin (Boko Haram). Each region presents unique challenges and opportunities for IS.

4. Al-Qaeda's Evolution: Al-Qaeda has adapted its strategies in response to changing circumstances, such as the 2011 Arab uprisings and competition with IS. Some al-Qaeda affiliates have exhibited pragmatism, caution in avoiding civilian casualties, and sensitivity to local norms.

The Evolving Landscape of Jihadism: A Comparative Analysis of IS and Al-Qaeda

In a recent conversation, Crisis Group's Libya Senior Analyst Claudia Gazzini shared her key findings with Hugh Pope regarding the presence of the Islamic State (IS) in Libya. IS is driven by the ambition to expand its influence beyond its regional stronghold by establishing provinces (wilayat) through aggressive recruitment and attracting other like-minded groups. This expansionist approach is notably less discerning than al-Qaeda, which tends to be more selective when accepting new affiliates. The group has had some success in various regions, although its achievements pale compared to its stronghold in Iraq, which is unsurprising given its strong Iraqi identity and historical roots there.

In Libya, specifically around the coastal town of Sirte, once a stronghold of the Qadhafi regime, IS managed to recruit from the local Ansar al-Sharia branch, exploiting a security vacuum. Despite having only a few hundred fighters, IS gained ground by striking deals with local leaders who had no other sources of protection. This region had no significant militias, as most residents were former regime loyalists "defeated" in the 2011 war. By 2015, IS had secured control over a 200-300km coastal stretch between Sirte and Ben Jawwad. The number of IS emissaries increased after June 2015, including Libyan returnees from Syria and foreign fighters, notably Iraqi IS commanders.

It is important to note that Libya does not have the same sectarian fault lines as Iraq or Syria. However, IS can exploit rifts between the state and communities associated with the former regime. In other parts of Libya, IS has not made significant progress. It has a limited, static presence in Benghazi, where it is believed to have coordinated with the Shura Council of Benghazi Revolutionaries, a mostly non-jihadist coalition fighting against forces commanded by General Khalifa Haftar. IS has been pushed out of Derna, another city with a history of jihadist activity, where Ansar al-Sharia and some al-Qaeda-linked groups dominate. Although Libya's chaotic and fluid militia scene is more challenging for IS to exploit, specific dynamics, such as rifts between the state and communities associated with the former regime, are evident.

IS in Egypt

In Egypt's Sinai region, Ansar Bayet al-Maqdis (ABM), a primarily Bedouin group, pledged allegiance to IS in November 2014. IS-Sinai recruits mainly locally but can draw on militants from the Nile Valley and conduct significant attacks in that region, including in Cairo. In north-eastern Sinai, it has posed a significant challenge to the Egyptian military through truck bombings, the widespread use of improvised explosive devices (IEDs), and large-scale battles in towns. Some of its expertise may have been imported from veterans of Syria or Iraq. IS-Sinai possesses advanced weaponry, including using MANPADS (man-portable air defence systems) in 2014 and Russian-made anti-tank Kornet missiles in 2015. The group also claimed responsibility for downing a Russian civilian airliner in October 2015.

IS in Yemen

In Yemen, IS emerged in November 2014, competing with a well-established and robust al-Qaeda movement. Despite this competition, some former al-Qaeda members and other militants pledged loyalty to IS, including Jalal Mohsen Saeed Baleedi, a former AQAP member from Abyan, who was killed in a suspected U.S. drone strike in February 2016. IS appears firmer in Hadramout, Aden, and Lahj, with a growing presence in Abyan, and is more brutal and less concerned about local norms and forging alliances than al-Qaeda. However, it recruits from the disillusioned and impoverished youth in the southern parts of Yemen. IS has also targeted the holy sites of Zaydis, a Shiite sect to which the Huthis belong, to stoke sectarian divisions and position itself as the protector of Sunnis. While fighting in Yemen is not solely along sectarian lines, deepening sectarian polarization could play into IS's hands.

IS in Afghanistan

Some former Pakistani Taliban commanders, traditionally held more sectarian views than their Afghan counterparts, established IS in Afghanistan's easternmost provinces. Throughout 2015, splinter groups from the Taliban occasionally aligned with IS for various reasons. However, the Taliban conglomerate remains the dominant armed opposition force, rooted in parts of Pashtun society and expanding its reach in the north. IS's Salafi-jihadist ideology alienates the Deobandi and rural Pashtun traditions the insurgency draws from, making it less appealing to Taliban leaders. Nevertheless, the Taliban leaders take the IS threat seriously, as the declaration of the caliphate and Baghdadi's claim to be the "commander of the faithful" directly challenged the legitimacy of the Taliban's emirate and Mullah Omar. Recent Taliban successes in the northeast and the southern heartlands have solidified support for Mullah Mansour, but this could weaken if he chooses, under Pakistani pressure, to pursue a negotiated settlement.

IS in Russia

By mid-2015, most of Russia's North Caucasus insurgency, known as the Caucasus Emirate, had pledged allegiance to Baghdadi. IS subsequently announced the creation of its "Wilayat Kavkaz." However, the Caucasus branch has suffered significant losses since Russian security services cracked down in 2013. The allure of fighting in Syria and a lack of anticipated financial support from Raqqa drove many Russian jihadists to the Levant. Militants in the North Caucasus have not received the support they expected from IS. Thus, the Caucasus region appears less of a priority for IS than Libya or South Asia, even though IS fighters with roots in the region often call for attacks against the Russian state in its name.

IS in the Chad Basin

Boko Haram's decision to pledge allegiance to IS in March 2015 seems partly motivated by Shekau's desire for publicity and the legitimacy of connecting his movement to the global jihad. However, this pledge only significantly altered the organization's capabilities, tactics, and identity beyond more sophisticated online promotion. There is no clear evidence of operational ties between Boko Haram and IS in Raqqa. While Boko Haram includes some foreign fighters, they are less numerous than other African jihadist movements. Boko Haram continues to cause significant suffering in its regions, but directly linking it to the global jihadist movement may misrepresent the nature of the threat it poses.

Understanding Al-Qaeda's Strategic Evolution

Al-Qaeda's strategic evolution, as documented in communications between affiliate leaders and demonstrated on the ground, reflects a pragmatic response to new opportunities and the need to adapt in the wake of the 2011 Arab uprisings, which initially appeared to render it obsolete. This shift in strategy may also be attributed to leadership changes within al-Qaeda, particularly the ascension of Ayman al-Zawahiri and the division with IS, which allowed al-Qaeda to distance itself from more extreme tactics. While Zarqawi's experience and the Anbar Awakening taught IS to show even less mercy to potential rivals, some al-Qaeda local branches appear to have drawn different conclusions. These branches prioritize pragmatism in their interactions with other militant groups and local communities, exercise caution in avoiding casualties among Muslims, and show greater sensitivity to local norms and public opinion.

IS and al-Qaeda share standard theological foundations but differ significantly in tactics, strategies, and goals. IS's rapid expansion, brutality, and recruitment methods pose a formidable challenge to regional stability, while al-Qaeda's affiliates exhibit greater pragmatism and adaptability. While al-Qaeda and IS theoretically share a broad interpretation of takfir, their actions diverge significantly. Al-Qaeda has traditionally attempted to minimize harm to fellow Muslims. For instance, Abu Musab al-Zarqawi's targeting of Shia in Iraq represented a departure from this norm, fueled by his hatred towards Shia, Iraq's emerging battle lines, and the perception of Iran's growing influence. The concept of takfir justified, for those who subscribed to it, a full-fledged Sunni offensive against Iran's perceived proxies in Baghdad.

Zarqawi's approach was further shaped by the ideas of new jihadist thinkers, who drew from non-Islamic traditions. For instance, Abu Bakr al-Naji, writing under a pseudonym, outlined in his work "Management of Savagery" how to create and exploit widespread violence to overthrow a tyrant and consolidate power. Abu Abdullah al-Muhajir, building on the work of others, including some with al-Qaeda links like Abu Yahya al-Libi, elaborated on these ideas, advocating specific tactics like suicide bombings, collateral damage, kidnapping, assassinations, and beheadings. These writers endorsed violence to protect marginalized Sunni communities, reshape society, and provide purpose to a generation oppressed by decades of authoritarian rule and an unfavourable global order.

At least in its propaganda, IS aims to eliminate the "grey zone," which it defines as any space of neutrality between the caliphate and heretical regimes and Western powers. Local IS commanders have occasionally shown pragmatism in Iraq and Syria, and they are likely to do so elsewhere, recognizing that eradicating all forms of Sunni opposition is unrealistic. Al-Qaeda and its affiliates have responded differently to popular uprisings. AQAP and al-Nusra may participate in sectarian conflicts and target Huthis and Alawites, and al-Qaeda does not hesitate to kill civilians or cooperate with deeply sectarian allies, as seen in Pakistan. However, leaders like Ayman al-Zawahiri, following the tradition of Osama bin Laden, tend to argue against making enemies of Shia and alienating Muslim public opinion through indiscriminate violence, which was evident when some al-Qaeda supporters celebrated AQIM's relative restraint during the November 2015 Bamako attack compared to IS's indiscriminate attacks in Paris a week earlier (though some non-Western Muslims were among the casualties in Bamako and Ouagadougou). Al-Qaeda in Syria and Yemen has worked with militias backed by powers it aims to overthrow and has occasionally received support from states.

The Distinction Between Near and Far Enemies

The distinction between "near" and "far" enemies has also evolved. While al-Qaeda initially shifted from targeting "heretical" states in the region to the West in the late 1990s, most of its affiliates now focus on local conflicts. In contrast, IS, initially as AQI and in its current form, primarily concentrated on Iraq, Syria, and other parts of the Muslim world. However, it appears to have shifted recently from merely encouraging "lone wolf" attacks elsewhere to actively dedicating resources for attacks against the West, as seen in its coordination of the Paris attacks, which is partly aimed at sowing discord within Western societies and provoking a backlash against the Muslim diaspora, which would help recruit more supporters and establish itself as the leader of the jihadist movement.

At the highest level, both IS and al-Qaeda have transnational goals. While their primary identity may relate to a specific region, such as Iraq or Yemen, they view their local struggles as part of a broader transnational jihad. In contrast, some movements with nationalist objectives focus on issues like removing an illegitimate government, opposing foreign "occupiers," or establishing their version of Sharia. They may not advocate political or religious pluralism, and while they may seek to govern within existing borders, their ideologies can vary.

Identifying the goals of these groups can be challenging. Official messaging may not necessarily reflect the beliefs of rank-and-file members or leadership. Some groups may espouse radical ideals to gain donors' favour or appear more pragmatic in their quest for state backing. Nevertheless, understanding their objectives, especially concerning the nation-state system, power-sharing, and tolerance for other sects or religious groups, is crucial for shaping effective policies and strategies. Any signs of ideological evolution or the potential for influence or division within these groups could open new avenues for mitigating their threat.

Jihadism and the Challenge Maturing to Statehood

Controlling a territory sustainably, albeit a formidable task for any insurgency, has proven exceptionally challenging for jihadist groups. Their strict and often harsh implementation of Sharia law has generally failed to garner widespread support. Observing strict Sharia laws cannot possibly support a peaceful or stable nation-state even where all the citizens are Muslims. Efforts by some jihadist groups to govern have failed due to excessive curtailing of citizens' freedoms, especially about women/girls. Jihadists have only found limited acceptance among communities that view them as the lesser of evil than total statelessness.

In recent history, few radical Islamist movements held territory before 2011. For example, the Taliban, as it expanded north and later governed most of Afghanistan in the mid-1990s, initially brought some degree of order. However, many were alienated by their puritanical policies, economic mismanagement, conscription, and atrocities. Similarly, al-Shabaab's rule during its territorial control (2007-2011) in Somalia brought some initial order but was characterized by extreme austerity. While some villagers initially welcomed services like Quranic education and primary medical care, these groups' violence, music bans, and other repressive measures eventually eroded their popularity.

Nonetheless, in the face of state collapse or extreme violence, some communities have accepted jihadist rule as the lesser evil, especially when jihadist groups provide essential services, predictable dispute resolution, and a semblance of law and order. For example, the Taliban's often swift and enforced justice system has earned some support, particularly in rural areas. In addition, the Taliban has occasionally allowed government health and education services in areas under their control.

Al-Shabaab, too, has pragmatically balanced violence with political acumen and mediation between clans. It has sometimes permitted humanitarian aid organizations to operate in controlled areas. These groups exert authority through coercion and co-option tailored to each situation.

More recently, IS and AQAP have demonstrated an evolving approach to governance in Iraq, Syria, and Yemen. Despite its brutal tactics and draconian implementation of Sharia, IS has shown an ability to run a state, co-opting parts of the local bureaucracy and maintaining functioning infrastructure and services. Its law enforcement has been strict but reportedly not corrupt, and it generates revenue through taxes. Some cities and towns allow government ministries to run schools and clinics. AQAP, too, has adapted its governance approach, learning from past mistakes and coordinating with local councils and aid organizations. It has provided effective dispute resolution essential public services and even engaged with representatives of Western aid organizations.

While these developments do not necessarily mean these groups are popular or credible alternatives in reasonably functioning states, they pose policy challenges. As more jihadist movements gain territory, questions arise about whether they can be contained geographically, allowing local communities time to revolt or support their ouster. Alternatively, will they successfully hold territory, provide services, and deepen their ties to communities, furthering their agendas and establishing safe havens for launching attacks? It remains too early to provide definitive answers. However, the fact that more jihadist groups control territory now than in the past, coupled with the persistence of crises that enable territorial gains, underscores the importance of monitoring these developments and their potential policy implications. Understanding how these groups govern, evolve, and interact with local populations is crucial for devising effective strategies to counter their influence and activities.

Review Questions

1. What are the critical differences in recruitment strategies between IS and Al-Qaeda, and how do they affect their respective expansionist approaches?
2. How did IS gain control over certain areas in Libya, and what factors contributed to its recruitment success there?
3. In which regions has IS been particularly active, and what tactics has it

employed to challenge local authorities and expand its influence?

4. How has Al-Qaeda evolved its strategies in response to changing geopolitical dynamics, and what distinguishes its approach from IS?

5. What challenges do jihadist groups face when attempting to govern territories, and how have they adapted their governance styles in recent years?

Discussion Points

1. Explore the reasons behind the different approaches of IS and Al-Qaeda in recruitment and expansion. How do these differences impact their effectiveness and longevity?

2. Discuss the governance challenges jihadist groups face when they control territories. How do their strict interpretations of Sharia law and economic policies affect local populations and their support?

3. Analyze the role of pragmatism in the strategies of some al-Qaeda affiliates. How do their efforts to avoid civilian casualties and build alliances with local communities affect their goals and objectives?

4. Consider the potential policy implications of jihadist groups gaining and holding territory. What are the risks and opportunities for containment, conflict resolution, and counterterrorism efforts?

5. Examine the concept of the "grey zone" in the context of IS's strategy. How does IS aim to eliminate this zone, and what are the consequences for Western societies and Muslim diasporas?

CHAPTER FIFTEEN: COMPLEXITIES OF COUNTERING THE FOURTH WAVE OF JIHADISM

Summary of Chapter Fifteen

1. Challenges in Countering Jihadism: Traditional counter-terrorism measures need to be revised in dealing with the fourth wave of Jihadism, as these groups control territories, provide public services, and generate local revenue. Geopolitical factors, differing perceptions of the threat, and state fragility exacerbate the complexity.

2. Addressing Root Causes: Countering jihadist groups requires addressing regional conflicts and rivalries fueling their growth. Promoting peace agreements, reducing regional rivalries, and building capable, resilient states is crucial.

3. Military Offensive Challenges: Military offensives against jihadist groups should be carefully considered, as they can lead to unintended consequences. A more patient and containment-focused approach is suggested to prevent military actions from strengthening these groups.

4. Engagement and Conflict Prevention: Engaging with jihadist groups, even discreetly, presents challenges but can be a valuable tool for conflict resolution. Preventing crises and violent extremism requires a comprehensive approach beyond the Countering Violent Extremism (CVE) agenda.

Countering the Fourth Wave of Jihadism

In recent years, jihadist movements have strengthened, posing a more significant challenge than ever before. Traditional counter-terrorism tools like designations, financial sanctions, travel bans, targeted killings, and special forces operations are insufficient when dealing with groups that control entire cities, towns, and supply lines, provide public services, generate local revenue, and maintain tens of thousands of fighters. Some of their leaders' ideological positions and aspirations further complicate political engagement. There is little modern precedent for defeating deeply entrenched insurgent movements through military means alone. Strategies that may have been effective in one context, like Sri Lanka's approach to the Tamil insurgency, may not work in regions characterized by porous borders, proxy wars, and states with limited control over their hinterlands. Replicating Russia's scorched-earth tactics in Chechnya in Syria is unlikely to defeat IS and may even bolster its ranks. Military gains in other areas have often led to the relocation of the jihadist problem rather than its eradication.

What makes the fourth wave particularly dangerous is the strength of these groups and the geopolitical upheaval they exploit. To effectively counter them, several key factors must be addressed:

Ending Regional Conflicts

Resolving the underlying causes of a conflict will make the environment less attractive to Jihadist groups. For example, in Yemen, ousting al-Qaeda from territories it controls is unlikely without a peace agreement between the Huthis, loyalists of former President Saleh, and forces aligned with the Saudi-led coalition. Prolonged chaos provides fertile ground for al-Qaeda to thrive. Even with a peace deal, the group's local connections may need to be more profound, and Yemeni security forces may be too weakened to oust violent jihadists. In Libya, reversing jihadist gains hinges on resolving rivalries among local factions and giving Qadhafi-era areas a stronger position in the national framework. While targeted airstrikes could disrupt IS operations, lasting success depends on collaboration among its enemies. Foreign military intervention should be considered carefully, without imposing it on the fledgling unity government, to avoid diminishing its credibility. Engaging with diverse Libyan security actors can also build support for the political process and identify potential partners against IS.

Addressing Regional Rivalries

A grand bargain is needed to counter IS effectively to de-escalate the Iran-Saudi Arabia rivalry, which fuels Sunni and Shia radicalism and poses a more significant threat to global stability than jihadists. The recent Chinese initiative to unite Iran and Saudi Arabia under the enlarged BRICS platform is thus a welcome development for addressing global Jihadism. The risk of mounting confrontations, especially in Syria, where both sides label their violence as counter-terrorism, could have severe consequences. Reducing other fault lines, such as those between conservative Arab regimes and the Muslim Brotherhood or Turkey and Kurdish armed groups, should also be pursued, even if reconciliation appears distant.

Addressing State Fragility

Many jihadist groups have filled vacuums left by state collapse in various regions. Building capable, resilient states is fundamental to countering extremism. However, prospects for recovery, reform, and regeneration, particularly in the Arab world, appear bleak. Governments responsible for the fourth wave often need help to adapt as needed to address the issue effectively.

Differing Perceptions of Threat

Leaders in affected countries may perceive the threat differently than their Western counterparts. Some may prioritize regional rivalries or fear that action against jihadists would anger religious establishments. Others may view opposition movements as a more significant threat to their rule or consider jihadists valid leverage with the West. The varying targets of jihadists, ranging from Western powers to local regimes and Shia populations, mean governments in affected areas face different dilemmas from Western powers. Balancing crackdowns can stir unrest, redirect jihadist anger at foreign powers domestically, and increase local terrorism, leading to fragile anti-jihadist alliances.

There is no one-size-fits-all solution to address jihadist groups, as each situation requires a case-by-case approach. Key considerations include assessing the group's strength, goals, community relationships, local grievances, government motivations, military capabilities, and the existence of credible local forces that can act without exacerbating the situation.

Countering IS in Iraq and Syria

IS's appeal partly lies in its perception of unstoppable momentum and its claim to Sunni leadership in the region. Therefore, it is crucial to prioritize efforts to oust or weaken IS in Iraq and Syria. However, it is essential to recognize that IS thrives in situations of chaos. Its narrative blends relentless advancement and apocalyptic visions of a final confrontation with Western forces. Additionally, it emerges from the suffering of Sunnis, particularly in Iraq, who struggled to find a new political identity after Saddam Hussein's removal. Reclaiming territory from IS is essential, but it should not further alienate Sunnis who have already felt marginalized after the 2003 invasion and subsequent betrayals such as the Awakening movement.

Mere airstrikes will not suffice. Disrupting IS's service delivery can harm communities and may even lead them to support local oppressors against external attackers. As seen in Raqqa after the Paris attacks, heavy bombardment lacks strategic value and may strengthen extremists while displacing more residents from their homes. Airstrikes can effectively support ground allies, raising questions about which forces can lead offensives.

Even when the U.S. troops in Iraq were around 160,000, success against IS required collaboration with local forces, which was still tricky; during the Awakening movement, the U.S. assisted the tribal "Sons of Iraq" by providing structure, rudimentary training, and financial support, and interference with the Iraqi state.

However, replicating such efforts today is challenging for various reasons. Even limited Western deployments, advocated by some, could inadvertently bolster IS's narrative of infidel crusaders, attracting more recruits. Russian involvement in Syria poses risks of global escalation. In Iraq, concerns arise due to Iran's influence and Shia politics in Baghdad. Furthermore, securing local and regional forces to support a Western presence is a complex task. In Syria, the anti-IS fight has been led by other rebel groups and their al-Qaeda affiliates, but they face significant challenges in the east while battling both the regime and Russian airstrikes. In Iraq, capable forces like Kurdish and Shia militias may not have local support in Sunni areas, which could further alienate these communities. Arming militias also weakens the Iraqi state.

Securing another Sunni uprising akin to the Awakening is unlikely. Tribal groups joined the fight against al-Qaeda in Iraq (AQI) only when they believed the U.S. would be a reliable partner. Their experience makes it difficult for foreign forces to gain their trust. With a substantial, open-ended commitment of troops, it will be easier to win back former allies.

Given the unlikelihood of a U.S. re-invasion, the current campaign against IS has been conducted on a more limited scale. Recent offensives involve evacuating civilians from towns, followed by massive airstrikes and joint efforts with local and regional forces to regain territory. Some Sunni political leaders displaced by IS await the opportunity to rebuild their authority and infrastructure to regain legitimacy.

However, this strategy may fail. Iran and Russia oppose any devolution of power that could empower Sunnis. Decentralization should be defined along administrative lines rather than sectarian ones to overcome Iranian resistance and offer flexibility to other provinces. Moreover, addressing the Sunni community's grievances and alienation, on which IS feeds, is essential. Building trust between Sunni leadership and constituents, especially the youth, is crucial for dislodging non-ideological supporters from IS's core.

Instead of attempting to replicate strategies used in the past, such as the 2015 capture of Tikrit and Ramadi, which resulted in the destruction of cities, a more patient and containment-focused approach might be advisable. This approach would slow the battle tempo, allowing political strategies to catch up and facilitate greater outreach before launching offensives. It starts by limiting bombings to vital targets and imminent threats, preventing IS expansion, and applying other pressure points to erode its aura of invincibility.

Containment, while a significant gamble given IS's ability to carry out attacks worldwide, could reduce the risks of undesirable outcomes, such as Iran taking the lead in combatting IS or IS surviving and consolidating its rule. However, it also involves political costs, including domestic criticism of appearing indecisive or ineffective. Despite these challenges, military escalation without a comprehensive political strategy is unlikely to be successful.

Approaches in Other Regions

Challenges in dealing with IS extend beyond Iraq and Syria, as other groups pose similar dilemmas. The approach to countering these groups must consider their potency, local connections, and the capacity of forces that can engage them.

For example, early Pakistani operations against militants sheltering al-Qaeda in tribal areas in 2002, mainly under U.S. pressure, proved disastrous. The military stirred up resistance, repeatedly retreated, and ceded more authority to militants through deals. While subsequent offensives have shown some progress, they continue to result in significant civilian casualties. In Nigeria, the initial response to Boko Haram ranged from denial to brutal crackdowns and air assaults, causing civilian deaths and mistrust toward troops outside the north. Corruption, logistical issues, and poor leadership plagued the efforts. Even now, more competent Nigerian and Chadian operations tend to be heavy-handed and indiscriminate while successfully reversing Boko Haram's gains. In Egypt's Sinai, operations against IS risk similar problems as collateral damage increases, and the population suffers under challenging conditions with little government relief.

Supporting Local Militias Against Extremist Groups

Supporting local militias against extremist groups poses its problems. In Pakistan and Nigeria, arming militias yielded short-term benefits but caused long-term issues. Arming anti-Taliban militias in Afghanistan entrenched predatory local forces and patronage networks, fueling support for the insurgency. Foreign boots on the ground come with their challenges as well. While some operations have been successful, like the French Serval operation in Mali, they cannot guarantee long-term stability. The 2003 Iraq invasion, for example, revitalized the global jihadist movement. In Afghanistan, U.S.-backed forces initially ousted the Taliban but now face a resurgent insurgency.

Withdrawal from conflict zones can also lead to worsening situations, such as the rise of IS after the U.S. departure from Iraq. In Somalia, foreign forces have inadvertently fueled radicalization. Combining centralized state-building with counter-insurgency often neglects reconciliation and improved governance, causing difficulties in defeating groups like the Taliban or al-Shabaab. Additionally, military aid often feeds corruption.

While military action is sometimes necessary, mainly to prevent expansion and atrocities, it should be part of a broader strategy. Wars are rarely simply battles between governments and extremists and often involve

Military Offensive Against Jihadists

The past decade has witnessed numerous states using military offensive to dislodge Jihadists. There is often a failure to consider its broader consequences adequately. It is important to emphasize that the ability of jihadists to shield themselves from government crackdowns, other militias, or foreign intervention is more pivotal to their success than their ideological beliefs. While they commit horrific acts of violence, it is essential to acknowledge that amid these conflicts, many extremists still find their way to win the hearts and minds of the local people who may be motivated to shield them from the state forces. Moreover, it is often the case that state forces violate international laws while going after extremists, and thus cause their actions to lose legitimacy. Military action should be well thought out, and the consequences should be analyzed before initiating.

Limited Efficacy of Targeted Killings

Targeted killings are only as effective as the strategy guiding their implementation. They can disrupt extremist networks and potential threats to Western nations, especially when deployed through drones that minimize immediate risks to military personnel. Notably, they have successfully dismantled al-Qaeda in the Pakistani tribal regions and appear to have hindered the operational capabilities of ISIS in Afghanistan. These strikes can also impede the movements of extremist leaders and exert psychological pressure on their groups. However, their most significant strength is also their greatest weakness. Drone strikes can destabilize local political situations and stoke resentment by shifting the asymmetrical nature of warfare to an extreme, where all risks fall on the targeted population, including civilians, and not on the attackers. Unless integrated into a comprehensive strategy to de-escalate conflicts, the tactical gains from targeted killings come at a significant cost.

Outside of Pakistan, targeted killings have a less pronounced impact on militant groups. In Yemen, where drone strikes have long been a central component of U.S. policy against AQAP, they have eliminated leaders like al-Wuhayshi and Ansar al-Awlaki, a prominent al-Qaeda ideologue. However, AQAP has endured, and collateral civilian casualties have fueled anger, especially among tribes whose support against al-Qaeda is crucial, thus nurturing anti-Western sentiment, if not direct support for jihadists.

In Somalia, the U.S. has killed commanders, including al-Shabaab's military chief, Aden Hashi Farah Ayro (2008), and its leader Ahmed Abdi Godane (2015). However, successors quickly emerged, and the transition from Ayro to Godane may have contributed to the group's radicalization as efforts were expedited to align with al-Qaeda. In other instances, more hardline commanders have replaced assassinated leaders, such as Hakimullah Mehsud in the Pakistani Taliban and Abubakar Shekau in Boko Haram. During the Afghan and Iraqi surges, killing mid-level commanders seems to have brought in a more radical and brutal generation. While this may strain the relationship between insurgents and communities, the strategy of eliminating leaders in hopes of radicalizing groups, which would then alienate communities and be won over later, appears frail, given the track records of state and foreign forces in these regions.

In summary, targeted assassinations can disrupt the operations of leaders and groups, but their predictability is low, and the risks are high. In the case of large insurgent movements in war zones, particularly well-organized groups like ISIS, a replacement, potentially more radical, often emerges quickly. Furthermore, ongoing infighting among jihadist groups, as seen with al-Qaeda and others confronting ISIS in various regions, further diminishes the impact of such actions. Little evidence suggests that targeted killings will end the conflicts these jihadist groups are involved in or decisively weaken their movements.

The Case for Engagement

Engaging with groups affiliated with IS and al-Qaeda, whether for hostage negotiations, humanitarian access, or the cessation of violence, presents practical and substantive challenges. Mediators face physical risks, and these movements' obscure hierarchies and structures complicate negotiations. Moreover, leaders' views may differ from those of frontline fighters. Resistance from states that have suffered attacks can also hinder engagement efforts. Legal obstacles come into play, with some states prohibiting support for groups designated as terrorists in ways that might penalize dialogue. In contrast, others ban facilitating the transportation of their representatives to safe meeting locations.

At times, negotiations have inadvertently emboldened movements with limited popular support. For example, in the Pakistani tribal areas, peace deals with various Taliban factions backfired, leading to further concessions and more authority granted to these groups until they posed a significant threat. However, in hindsight, the U.S. rejection of confident Taliban leaders' offers in 2001 to accept the new order in exchange for government positions or safety appears unwise. While such engagement might not have prevented all forms of insurgency, it could have shaped the nature of the insurgency differently. Currently, Kabul and its foreign allies may have to make substantial concessions to persuade the Taliban to cease hostilities, assuming the group intends to do so without fragmenting.

Reluctance to engage with jihadists has led to missed opportunities, as demonstrated in the case of al-Shabaab. In Mali, involving Ansar Dine leader Iyad ag-Ghali in the peace process, though challenging, might have increased the chances of peace in Kidal. The Mali peace agreement also failed to address the role of religion in politics, a crucial factor that could have undermined support for radical groups by addressing one of their primary demands. Efforts to encourage Ansar al-Sharia leaders in Libya to embrace democracy were showing promise but were derailed by escalating violence.

Similarly, after the 2009 crackdown in Maiduguri, Boko Haram called for the restoration of its mosque and accountability for its leader's killing. Engagement would have been challenging, but these demands could have served as a starting point. Instead, both sides escalated, leading to the proliferation of Boko Haram into a regional threat. The Nigerian government should continue offering dialogue to members willing to engage, aiming to counter the movement's narrative of a cruel and oppressive state while seeking pragmatic factions that can be brought into the fold. It should also bring those responsible for Yusuf's death to justice and release the imprisoned wives of Boko Haram leaders. However, achieving a mediated settlement with the group's radical and increasingly nihilistic core remains remote.

Refusing to engage with jihadists in principle seems outdated, given their prominence, community ties, and the mixed results of military actions against them while pursuing efforts to weaken their support through improved governance. Some movements previously deemed "irreconcilable" are already engaged discreetly, such as the Afghan Taliban, and the same applies to parts of al-Shabaab. In some cases, even groups affiliated with al-Qaeda may offer opportunities for engagement due to their territorial control, coordination with aid organizations, and ties to state-backed armed groups.

Contact with many groups should be pursued without unrealistic expectations of their immediate departure from global jihad or transition to peaceful political participation. The prospects are generally more favourable with groups with national objectives and even more so with those willing to embrace pluralism. Governments may only sometimes be best suited for direct engagement. However, policymakers can leverage existing contacts and ongoing efforts by community leaders, non-state mediators, and humanitarian organizations, especially in Western capitals. These entities can provide insights into the dynamics within these groups, facilitate humanitarian access, and alleviate suffering. While many jihadist movements have committed heinous acts against civilians, addressing these crimes through transnational justice is crucial rather than allowing them to dictate decisions regarding engagement.

Mediators face a range of questions: What is the purpose of engagement? What are the associated risks? Could it empower hardliners at the expense of more moderate elements? Might it incur costs with other actors? Who is best positioned to initiate engagement? Can it delegitimize the use of violence by those who do not participate? While the answers may vary, these questions apply equally to the most extreme groups as they do to any armed movement. Especially now, with various groups, including those with transnational and national objectives, prominently involved in conflicts, it is essential to monitor them as significant players rather than merely threats to the West. The door to engagement should be left ajar, and policymakers should be prepared to identify and assess prospects for dialogue as opportunities arise.

Preventing Crises or Preventing Violent Extremism?

The recent expansion of groups linked to IS and al-Qaeda adds urgency to conflict prevention efforts, particularly in regions stretching from West Africa to South Asia. Since these movements are likely to exploit any new crisis, and the chances of reversing their gains or ending conflicts diminish once they establish themselves, bolstering the resilience of vulnerable states still standing is imperative. While appearing stable on the surface, many of these states are fragile beneath.

The emerging Countering Violent Extremism (CVE) agenda is expected to play a role in this effort, although its precise contributions remain unclear. This agenda was initially conceived as a softer alternative to the militarized response to the 9/11 attacks, initially led by development organizations that recognized the limitations of a strategy solely based on military force. The CVE agenda typically includes actions such as community engagement, countering extremist narratives, preventing the flow of foreign fighters, and addressing the root causes of radicalization, often related to youth unemployment, poor governance, or oppressive regimes. Different states and the United Nations emphasize different aspects of CVE, with some focusing on ideology, others on the factors that attract individuals to extremist groups, and others on addressing radicalization's underlying causes. The UN Secretary-General's recent Plan of Action on Preventing Violent Extremism calls on member states to develop their action plans, which should incorporate measures addressing a wide range of sources of fragility.

Much of what the CVE agenda promotes is sensible. It is vital to acknowledge grievances that underlie the recruitment of extremists, the responsibilities of states, and the connections between radicalization and human rights abuses, repressive governance, thwarted aspirations, and marginalization. The plan also emphasizes the need for member states to respect human rights while responding to extremism. However, the plan stops short of explicitly linking the recent gains of jihadists to the policies of major regional and global powers in the Middle East, even though it recognizes that violent extremism does not emerge in isolation and calls for redoubled efforts to end protracted conflicts.

Since the fourth wave of Jihadism partly stems from the failures of securitized policies since 9/11, criticizing the CVE agenda, designed to address these failures, may seem ungrateful. However, there are potential pitfalls in relying on CVE as the primary framework for assessing threats to stability.

First, while recognizing the diverse factors contributing to extremism and reallocating resources to address them is valuable, framing these efforts solely through the CVE lens may be counterproductive. Creating employment opportunities for youth is essential, but it is not a universal preventive measure and may only deter some individuals from joining extremist groups under specific conditions. Addressing marginalized communities is essential, but doing so solely to gain their support against extremists, or, worse, conditioning development on their support, can work against the principles of aid and those delivering it. Education is a fundamental right for children and should not be reframed as a CVE tool, nor should it be used to distort the delivery of essential public services. Similarly, women activists should be engaged in policy development, not coerced into informing their children. Encouraging governments to adopt inclusive and gradual reforms is often the most valuable contribution allies can make in preventing crises that extremists could exploit. Labelling such diplomatic efforts as CVE does not add value.

Second, governments and the UN may not be the best entities to develop counter-narratives on religion, and co-opting religious leaders could weaken moderate imams. Governments should instead allow and protect space for diverse voices within the Muslim community, whether Salafi or otherwise. Furthermore, the role of ideology in driving the recent wave of extremism is not straightforward. While Salafist proselytizing and state-sponsored Islamization have set the stage in some regions, the fourth wave owes more to the exploitation of warfare and state collapse by jihadists or armed groups adopting extreme tactics as crises deepen than early-stage radicalization. During crises, support for extremists is often based less on shared values and more on what they provide when governance fails: protection from a despised regime, swift dispute resolution, social advancement, or profit opportunities.

While African and other leaders have valid concerns about unregulated Gulf funding for intolerant preachers, focusing on this issue to the detriment of other sources of fragility is short-sighted. The most likely scenario for IS or al-Qaeda-linked groups to gain a foothold in Chad is through a collapse of the state amid power struggles and resource conflicts. The same applies to other Lake Chad Basin states, Central Asia, and other regions. Measures against jihadists must avoid inadvertently increasing the likelihood of violent breakdown by supporting exclusive and destabilizing governance patterns.

Perhaps the most problematic aspect of the CVE agenda is the loose or absent definition of "violent extremist." Does it refer to specific doctrines, tactics, outreach efforts, or aspirations? Some Western governments use the label as a euphemism for the jihadists discussed in this report, while others apply it to various forms of Islamic militants like Hamas. Some even include violent right-wing movements in Europe.

This broad definition obscures more than it clarifies and risks conflating diverse forms of protest, rebellion, and radicalism under "violent extremism." If confusing the Taliban and al-Qaeda was a mistake fifteen years ago, creating a category that might include IS, Hamas, the FARC insurgents in Colombia, and right-wing extremists in the West is analytically flawed and could lead to policies that enable leaders to portray their adversaries as irreconcilable and lock their countries into endless conflicts against them. Even the movements discussed in this report, among the most extreme non-state armed groups today in terms of beliefs and goals, comprise a core dedicated to a specific ideology and many others fighting for various local and non-ideological reasons. Policymakers should differentiate between these movements and explore opportunities to end violence rather than lump them together.

The past decade has shown that violence can strengthen extremist groups or leave communities trapped in brutal conflicts. While effective in some cases, targeted killings often have unpredictable consequences and come at a high cost. Engagement with jihadist groups presents challenges but should not be ruled out, as it can potentially reveal opportunities for conflict resolution. Additionally, the CVE agenda has merit, but it should not overshadow other sources of fragility, and its definition of "violent extremism" needs refinement to avoid unwarranted categorizations. Ultimately, preventing crises and extremism requires a comprehensive approach that considers the complexities of each situation.

Review Questions

1. What are the limitations of traditional counter-terrorism tools in countering the fourth wave of Jihadism?
2. Why is addressing regional conflicts and rivalries essential in countering jihadist groups?
3. What are the challenges and potential risks associated with military offensives against jihadist groups?
4. How does engagement with jihadist groups fit into the strategy for conflict resolution?
5. What criticisms are raised regarding the Countering Violent Extremism (CVE) agenda, and why is a broader approach necessary?

Discussion Points

1. Discuss the role of regional conflicts and rivalries in the growth of jihadist groups. How can these be effectively addressed to counter extremism?
2. Explore the challenges and ethical considerations of engaging with jihadist groups for conflict resolution. What are the potential benefits and risks?
3. Compare and contrast the approaches to countering jihadist groups in Iraq and Syria with those in other regions mentioned in the text, such as Pakistan and Nigeria.
4. Examine the role of state fragility in allowing jihadist groups to thrive. How can states be supported in building resilience?
5. Consider the broader implications of a containment-focused approach to countering jihadist groups. What are the potential political, humanitarian, and security consequences?

CONCLUSION

In the book "Diplomacy, Extremism, and Development," the complex and ever-evolving global landscape is navigated by global interdependence, regional conflicts, and the persistent threat of violent extremism. This exploration illuminates the intersection of diplomacy, extremism, and development, revealing diplomacy's indispensable role in shaping a more peaceful, secure, and prosperous world.

Throughout the chapters, we have unfolded the layers of this multifaceted triad, examining the profound impact of diplomacy in addressing extremism and promoting development. The book demonstrates how diplomacy acts as a catalyst for cooperation, a mediator in conflicts, and a vehicle for international engagement. From preventive diplomacy to multilateral initiatives, cultural diplomacy, and economic cooperation, diplomacy has emerged as a powerful force for change in our interconnected world.

The primary causes of extremism – the economic disparities, social unrest, and political instability that fuel the flames of radicalization – and how they hinder development are explained. Remarkable success stories, where diplomacy, often alongside development efforts, has successfully resolved conflicts, diffused tensions and paved the way for lasting peace, are presented for readers to draw valuable lessons.

The complexities of firearms proliferation, the humanitarian crises in the Sahel region, and the far-reaching impact of transnational organized crime were discussed. In doing so, we have underscored the urgency of diplomacy in addressing these pressing global challenges, highlighting that the tools of negotiation, dialogue, and cooperation are essential in creating a safer and more just world.

Presented also are perspectives of influential figures on silencing the guns in Africa. Also discussed are adapting to the ever-changing landscape of jihadism and the strategic restructuring of Western counterterrorism architecture in response to Russia's attack on Ukraine. These insights remind us that the world is shaped not only by the actions of states but by the evolving dynamics of several factors, especially emerging threats and a growing number of non-state armed groups.

This book is not just another academic discourse on diplomacy, extremism, and development but a call to action. It beckons us to engage with the complexities of our time, embrace the principles of diplomacy, and seek solutions that prioritize peace, development, and the well-being of all. Uncertainty, challenges, and opportunities mark the future. The trends of digital diplomacy, preventive diplomacy, gender mainstreaming, and sustainable development offer glimpses of hope and progress. However, these trends require our active engagement, commitment to dialogue, and willingness to confront extremism with resilience and determination.

"Diplomacy, Extremism, and Development" can guide the journey toward a more peaceful and prosperous world. It reminds us that while the challenges are complex, the power of diplomacy to effect positive change is boundless. It encourages us to foster cooperation, address root causes, and advocate for peace and development as the ultimate antidote to extremism. We hope the insights from these pages will inspire everyone to engage with the world's complexities, champion diplomacy, and work towards a future where extremism recedes, development flourishes, and peace prevails. Together, we can shape a world where diplomacy reigns supreme, extremism withers, and development thrives.

AREAS FOR FURTHER RESEARCH AND STUDIES

"Diplomacy, Extremism, and Development" is a comprehensive exploration of a dynamic and evolving field at the intersection of diplomacy, security, and development. While it covers a broad spectrum of topics, there are several areas where further studies and research can provide valuable insights and expand our understanding. Here are some potential areas for future research:

1. Evaluation of Diplomatic Strategies: Conduct in-depth case studies and evaluations of specific diplomatic strategies, both successful and unsuccessful, in addressing extremism and fostering development. Analyze the impact, lessons learned, and potential adaptations for different contexts.

2. Soft Power Diplomacy: Investigate the role of soft power diplomacy, including cultural and educational diplomacy, in countering extremism and promoting development. Explore how countries can effectively utilize their cultural assets to influence narratives and build bridges.

3. Digital Diplomacy and Technology: Explore the evolving landscape of digital diplomacy, including social media and emerging technologies, in countering extremist propaganda and mobilizing support for development initiatives. Assess the challenges and opportunities of digital diplomacy in the 21st century.

4. Gender Diplomacy: Examine the role of gender mainstreaming in diplomacy and its impact on countering extremism and promoting gender-inclusive development. Investigate how gender-sensitive approaches can lead to more effective outcomes.

5. Climate Diplomacy: Analyze the connections between climate change, environmental degradation, and extremism and explore diplomatic efforts to address these interrelated challenges. Investigate how climate diplomacy can contribute to sustainable development and conflict prevention.

6. Diplomacy in the Fragile States: Focus on the specific challenges and strategies of diplomacy in fragile and conflict-affected states. Explore how diplomatic efforts can be tailored to address the unique dynamics of these environments.

7. Multilateral Diplomacy and International Cooperation: Assess the effectiveness of multilateral diplomacy in addressing global extremism and development challenges. Study the role of international organizations, alliances, and coalitions in promoting peace, security, and sustainable development.

8. Humanitarian Diplomacy: Investigate the evolving role of humanitarian diplomacy in conflict zones and crises. Analyze how humanitarian diplomacy can be leveraged to facilitate access to vulnerable populations and support development efforts.

9. Preventive Diplomacy: Explore the concept of preventive diplomacy in the context of extremism and conflict prevention. Assess the strategies, mechanisms, and early warning systems that can proactively address the root causes of violence.

10. Economic Diplomacy: Examine economic diplomacy as a tool for promoting development and countering extremist ideologies. Investigate the role of trade, investment, and economic cooperation in fostering stability and prosperity.

11. Peacebuilding and Conflict Transformation: Delve into the practical aspects of peacebuilding and conflict transformation through diplomatic means. Analyze case studies of successful peace agreements, reconciliation processes, and post-conflict development.

12. Human Rights and Diplomacy: Study the intersection of human rights, diplomacy, and extremism. Assess how diplomatic efforts can advance human rights protections, promote the rule of law, and prevent

radicalization.

13. Case Studies and Regional Analyses: Conduct in-depth regional analyses and case studies to understand the specific challenges and opportunities for diplomacy in countering extremism and promoting development in different parts of the world.

14. Measuring Impact: Develop methodologies and metrics for assessing the impact of diplomatic efforts in countering extremism and advancing development goals. Evaluate the long-term outcomes of diplomatic interventions.

15. Ethical and Normative Dimensions: Explore diplomacy's ethical and normative dimensions in addressing extremism and development. Consider the moral imperatives, principles, and values that guide diplomatic decision-making.

SOURCES

American Foreign Service Association. (n.d.). The global war on terror and diplomatic practice.https://afsa.org/global-war-terror-and-diplomatic-practice

Bjola, C., & Holmes, M. (2015). Digital Diplomacy: Theory and Practice. https://www.routledge.com/Digital-Diplomacy-Theory-and-Practice/Bjola-Holmes/p/book/9781138843820

Chiangi, M. A. (u.d). Critically Examining David Rapoport's Four Waves Theory of Modern Terrorism in the Light of Factual Historical Events. https://caert.org.dz/Publications/Articles/Article-1-vol-11-1.pdf

ooper, A. F., Heine, J., & Thakur, R. (2010). The Oxford Handbook of Diplomacy. https://academic.oup.com/edited-volume/34361

Council on Foreign Relations. (n.d.). Violent extremism in the Sahel. https://www.cfr.org/global-conflict-tracker/conflict/violent-extremism-sahel#:~:text=Current%20instability%20is%20associated%20with,1963%2C%201990%2C%20and%202006.

Cragin, K. (2003). Terrorism and Development: Using Social and Economic Development to Inhibit a Resurgence of Terrorism. https://www.rand.org/pubs/monograph_reports/MR1630.html

Hogg, M. A. (2015). Extremism and the Psychology of Uncertainty. https://www.researchgate.net/publication/264811518_Extremism_and_the_Psychology_of_Uncertainty

International Affairs. (n.d.). Preventing violent extremism through the United Nations: The rise and fall of a good idea. https://academic.oup.com/ia/article/94/2/251/4851908

International Crisis Group. (n.d.). Exploiting disorder: Al-Qaeda and the Islamic State.https://www.crisisgroup.org/global/exploiting-disorder-al-qaeda-and-islamic-state

Just Security. (n.d.). Letting diplomacy lead US counterterrorism: What would that look like?https://www.justsecurity.org/75046/letting-diplomacy-lead-us-counterterrorism-what-would-that-look-like/

Keefer, P., & Loayza, N. (2010). Terrorism, Economic Development, and Political Openness. https://www.cambridge.org/core/books/terrorism-economic-development-and-political-openness/B85CF1E3818EC683069CD03839583E1A

Moran, J., & Littler, M. (2016). Extremism, Counter-terrorism and Policing. https://www.jstor.org/stable/26626869

Muldoon Jr., J. P., Sullivan, E., Aviel, J. F., et al. (2005). Multilateral Diplomacy and the United Nations Today. https://www.jstor.org/stable/26626869

National Defense University. (n.d.). Brothers came back with weapons: The effects of arms proliferation from Libya.https://cco.ndu.edu/News/Article/1171858/brothers-came-back-with-weapons-the-effects-of-arms-proliferation-from-libya/

Organization for Economic Co-operation and Development (OECD). (2016). Preventing Violent Extremism through Inclusive Development. https://www.undp.org/sites/g/files/zskgke326/files/publications/Discussion%20Paper%20-%20Preventing%20Violent%20Extremism%20by%20Promoting%20Inclusive%20%20Development.pdf

ReliefWeb. (n.d.). Effective arms-control measures needed to block diversion of Ukraine weapons, senior United Nations disarmament official tells Security Council.https://reliefweb.int/report/ukraine/effective-arms-control-measures-needed-block-diversion-ukraine-weapons-senior-united-nations-disarmament-official-tells-security-council?gclid=EAIaIQobChMI9djN2uWxgQMVQtntCh0eVgasEAAYBCAAEgLMZ_D_BwE

ReliefWeb. (n.d.). Peace and proliferation: The Russo-Ukrainian war and the illegal arms trade. https://reliefweb.int/report/ukraine/peace-and-proliferation-russo-ukrainian-war-and-illegal-arms-trade-enuk?gclid=EAIaIQobChMIsYSXxuSxgQMVQeztCh1k5gZGEAAYASAAEgI7PPD_BwE

Sen, A. (1999). Development as Freedom. http://www.c3l.uni-oldenburg.

de/cde/OMDE625/Sen/Sen-intro.pdf

Sending, O. J. (2015). Diplomacy and the Making of World Politics. https://www.cambridge.org/core/books/diplomacy-and-the-making-of-world-politics/862A29BB9FD3EBF5DAE5508C7B55C0B6

Swiss Federal Department of Foreign Affairs. (n.d.). Preventing violent extremism (PVE).https://www.eda.admin.ch/eda/en/fdfa/foreign-policy/human-rights/peace/pve.html

United Nations. (2023). Root causes of conflicts in Africa must be addressed beyond traditional response, special adviser tells Security Council debate on silencing guns. https://press.un.org/en/2023/sc15249.doc.htm

United Nations Development Programme. (n.d.). Human Development Report. https://annualreport.undp.org/

UNODC. (n.d.). Indirect impacts of firearms on states or communities https://www.unodc.org/e4j/zh/firearms/module-1/key-issues/indirect-impacts-of-firearms-on-states-or-communities.html

UNODC. (n.d.). Transnational organized crime: The globalized illegal economy.https://www.unodc.org/toc/en/crimes/organized-crime.html

U.S. Department of State. (n.d.). United States strategy to prevent conflict and promote stability.https://www.state.gov/united-states-strategy-to-prevent-conflict-and-promote-stability/